SCRIPTURE
Talks

50 Creative Messages

for Youth

SCRIPTURE Talks

50 Creative Messages

for Youth

Contents

The CD–Rom features PowerPoint® presentations that accompany many of the talks. The mouse icons in the print versions of the talks indicate when the speaker should click to the next slide in the presentation.

Introduction

Moses was pretty sure he couldn't pull it off with a speech impediment like his; Jeremiah took one look at his peach-fuzzed face in the mirror and declared himself way too young; Isaiah's sweaty feet shook in his sandals at the thought of it; and if Hosea and Ezekiel had been given a heads-up on the wacky object lessons they'd be living in the middle of, they might have run while they had the chance. Being God's voice to a generation isn't a task to be taken lightly.

In fact, the absurdity of it all hits me every time I stand up in front of a group of youth to speak. Think about it! The Creator of the universe wants stuff to be said through YOU. It's life and death stuff; it's stuff that can be hard to understand, and even harder to explain; it's stuff that puts youth at the tough crossroads of decision-making; and incredibly, God chooses the likes of you and me to communicate this stuff. Shouldn't the Lord be afraid that the message could get garbled in the translation? Isn't God concerned that our lives are inconsistent with the message we proclaim? Doesn't the Almighty worry that we might get the message all wrong? These are all possibilities, but in spite of it we—inadequate, stuttering, under-equipped, inexperienced—get the responsibility of being God's spokespeople.

This book is all about learning from fellow stutterers how we can be more effective in communicating the most important message in history to the most important generation of our time—the good news of Jesus for Millennial students who are in the midst of shaping their values and beliefs and laying down the foundations on which they will build their adult lives. This book contains the thoughts of many youth workers who, like you, have faced the challenge of standing up in front of a group of youth to communicate the truth in a way that will connect deeply and effect change in the lives of those who listen.

I don't need to tell you that standing up in front teenagers as a "speaker" can be intimidating. We've all heard our youth's nasty critiques of other speakers who we thought did a pretty good job!

We've seen their glazed, daydreaming eyes staring vacantly at us when we just weren't connecting. The truth is: For many people giving a talk is as scary as it gets. In some surveys public speaking ranks higher on the terror scale than death itself (which means that at a funeral most people would rather be the one in the box than the one giving the eulogy!) Not only that, but the students to whom we're talking live in a multi-media world of vivid images, surround sound, and special effects. The fact that most of us are at least one generation removed from our audience cranks up the stress another notch. But in spite of the unique challenges, the huge responsibility, and the high stakes, the privilege is immense. We find ourselves in "front row seats" and see God at work firsthand.

Can You Relate?

"My people come to you, as they usually do, and sit before you to listen to your words, but they do not put them into practice. With their mouths they express devotion, but their hearts are greedy for unjust gain. Indeed, to them you are nothing more than one who sings love songs with a beautiful voice and plays an instrument well, for they hear your words but do not put them into practice."

—Ezekiel 33:31-32 (NIV)

Hopefully, you'll benefit from the generosity of the contributors who have shared their hard work with you in this book. You'll see each speaker's unique style and personality reflected in the way he or she approaches a topic. You'll sense the presenters' passion for truth, which they have carefully developed into messages for their students. You'll hear their sense of humor coming through in their anecdotes and illustrations. And you'll be invited to use their thoughts and ideas to shape your own talks for your group.

Some Thoughts on Speaking to Youth So They'll Listen

Let's get something straight right up front. God doesn't need skilled and polished orators to get a message across. God calls men and women whose lives are marked by integrity, honesty, and humility, and who are willing to thoughtfully present and then live out the truth. If we don't meet these prerequisites, we'll just be speaking our own words for our own purposes. Empty words don't carry much life-changing power! And kids can spot a phony pretty quickly. Youth simply won't listen to us if we lack credibility or come across as untrustworthy.

So as long as we're pretty sincere straight-shooters who love Jesus and genuinely care about youth, we'll be effective communicators. Right? Not necessarily. Speaking well also involves a commitment to skill development, practice, and self-critique. When we are speaking on behalf of the Creator of the universe, we need to take the responsibility pretty seriously.

Below are a few logistical suggestions for strengthening the talks you give to youth. These suggestions are not meant as inviolable rules, but rather as ideas that can enhance your effectiveness when you stand up to deliver your message.

Start Strong

Make sure you're ready to sprint out of the starting blocks. Know exactly what you want to say when you first open your mouth—it's a good idea to actually memorize your first few sentences or opening story. The first ninety seconds of your talk might well determine whether youth will listen to you. Youth often ask themselves, "Does this person have anything to say that I would be interested in hearing?" Remember, your audience comes from a generation of media surfers who feel no obligation to stay tuned in. They're used to changing channels in five seconds if something on the screen doesn't grab their attention, and they'll just as quickly tune out of a talk that doesn't feel like it's going anywhere.

Your opening should both set the tone of your talk and establish the direction in which you want to lead your listeners. Your opening is no time for apologies, fumbling for your notes, blowing into the microphone (if you use one), or commenting on your nervousness. Some well-delivered humor can help establish a rapport with the youth and ease your own nervousness; a humorous personal story is often more effective than a predictable cheesy joke or canned sermon illustration. More on that later.

Shoot for Short

Millennials rarely say, "I wish that talk had gone on and on a lot longer. I just can't get enough sub-points these days!" Good youth talks usually make **one** point well then suggest a practical response to what they've heard. Aside from the fact that young people have shorter attention spans than adults, there are other equally important reasons for keeping youth talks short and sharp:

1. Most of us already know the teens to whom we're speaking. So we will probably teach more effectively through relationships than from behind a music stand and microphone. The "talk" simply gives them something to relate to. Let's not forget that this generation listens with their eyes. Youth want to see you practice more and preach less.

2. Most talks end up being longer than they need to be because of poor preparation and planning. We've all suffered through talks littered with unplanned ad-libs, redundancy, and poorly told stories. Plan, prepare, say it well, and then sit down.

3. Many youth are simply incapable of responding to multiple points or complex ideas. The longer most talks go on, the more confusing they become and the less likely youth are to understand what they are being challenged to do. You can't make every point and serve every need in one talk. Relax! You will have other chances.

Land It!

Knowing how your talk will end is nearly as important as nailing the beginning. We've all heard speakers say "finally" or "let me wrap things up" and then circle around like a fog-bound plane for the next twenty minutes. When students sense that you've made your point and have "started your descent," their internal countdown timer starts ticking. Ending your talk confidently and clearly is important because your conclusion is where you want to answer the "so what?" question. Unlike the Choose Your Own Adventure™ books that some of your youth probably read when they were younger, a good talk needs just one ending. Decide what that ending will be and deliver it well. If you are asking for a tangible response—writing a letter to God, coming forward for prayer, filling out a response card, discussing with a neighbor, and so on—be sure that you have the necessary supplies and that you give clear instructions.

Work it Through Your Own Life First

Perhaps the greatest injustice we can do as speakers is to call youth to respond to a truth that we have not experienced ourselves. Because the book you are holding in your hands right now includes talks with lessons and stories that were originally lived and learned by someone else, you may have to make the extra effort to connect the talk to your own life experience. With relatively little preparation or thought you can lay down these points for a group of youth as though they've come right out of your own experience of God's word. Our youth know something about our lives, and if what we say doesn't match what they see, we will lose our credibility in a heartbeat. You can probably relate to what Paul said to his friends in Thessalonica: "So deeply do we care for you that we are determined to share with you not only the gospel of God but also our own selves, because you have become so dear to us" (1 Thessalonians 2:8).

This book is a resource for preparing your talks. It is not intended as a way to eliminate preparation time, but to make better use of it. If a message you deliver from this book goes into your eyes and out through your mouth without being intentionally filtered through your own heart and mind, it will likely sound hollow to your listeners and be an unsatisfactory experience for you.

Don't Fudge on the "So What?"

I have a large banner hanging over my office door. I stare at it as I sit at my desk and I can't leave the room without seeing it. The words on the banner are simply "So What?" This phrase is a constant reminder to me that unless my words call students to some sort of response or change I'm wasting my breath. My sense is that this is where youth workers most often drop the ball in our work with teenagers. We do a good job of picking topics that we know youth care about; we make sure they know the details about the biblical text; we illustrate our talks with engaging media clips or heart-grabbing stories; and then we fail to call youth to make life-changing choices in response to what they've heard. The whole point of giving a talk is application. If we can't get it into our youth's lives, we've missed the point completely.

Think about moving the message from head to heart to hands—from content to conviction to action! Many youth who hear our words have not moved past head knowledge of the Bible. They would do great on a multiple choice exam, but their lives have not been transformed. James says it well when he reminds us:

> Think about moving the message from head to heart to hands—from content to conviction to action!

"For if any are hearers of the word and not doers, they are like those who look at themselves in a mirror . . . and, on going away, immediately forget what they were like. But those who look into the perfect law . . . being not hearers who forget but doers who act—they will be blessed in their doing" (James 1:23–25).

"So What?" Topics

Effective speaking will call youth to make intentional changes in one of the following areas:

Behavior: A conscious commitment to start or stop doing something

Attitude: A change in the way one feels about something or someone

Perspective: An openness to looking at something from a completely new angle

Priorities: A willingness to make something less or more important

Relationships: A readiness to risk opening up to someone, or to willingly walk away

Habits: An elimination of life patterns that destroy, or an implementation of those that bring life

Just one more thing: If we are going to challenge youth to apply the truth of our messages to their lives, we must remember that they probably won't succeed alone. We can't just lay out a heavy "so what" challenge then walk away. Below is a list of what youth need from us as they act on what they're learning:

Support and Encouragement—Obedience to God's truth is often counter-cultural. Youth who take seriously God's word may be misunderstood and alienated by friends and family and may need extra support as they work through the implications of their new choices. These youth need someone to notice and affirm the changes in their lives. Following the truth may take them down a path that seems lonely.

- **Resources**—Some of the challenges we give our youth will require tools for implementation. If we encourage students to commit to thirty days of consistent Bible reading, we should prepare for them a thirty-day plan and give them a copy to keep in their Bibles. If we ask them to share their faith with a friend, we should help them prepare their faith story so that they can tell it with clarity and confidence. We want to help them be successful.
- **Accountability**—I sometimes wonder how youth feel when we passionately call them to specific actions in response to our teaching but never again mention this calling. Following up by asking youth how well they are meeting a certain challenge or by giving them a chance to talk about how they have responded to a certain message lets them know that we are serious about the challenge.
- **Patience, Forgiveness, Second Chances**—Adolescent behavior is often erratic. Thus youth may struggle to implement the changes we call them to. The passion they feel at the end of that retreat often quickly gives way to the realities of peer pressure, busyness, and adolescent immaturity. How we respond to their failures will help determine how willing youth are to try again.

Make it Yours!

One of the best ways to make these talks (or any talks for that matter) your own is to flavor them with stories. Jesus regularly used stories to drive home his point. Millennials are all about telling and hearing one another's stories. And they love to hear ours.

Make sure to tell your story well. Prepare your personal illustrations as carefully as you do the rest of your talk. Use your words to paint pictures and create an emotional response. Tell stories that illustrate both failure and success. If we only parade our victories, we'll discourage youth in their pursuit of spiritual growth. If we only talk about failure, we might lose our credibility. I like to think in terms of "ministry-motivated transparency": We choose to tell about certain parts of our lives, not because of what it does for us but for how it meets the needs of those who are listening.

Another option is to invite a student to share a testimony to illustrate a point. You know your youth well enough to recognize when a first person account of one of their experiences would be better than one of yours. Allowing them to contribute in this way will give them speaking experience but, more importantly, will validate their story and give other youth a chance to learn from one of their peers.

Some Ideas for Finding Your Own Stories

If you think you have no stories of your own, it may be because you haven't thought about some of these categories:

Injuries	Accidents
Sports	Dating
Pets	Embarrassing Moments
Birthdays	Puberty
Parents	Stupid Decisions
Sibling Rivalry	Family Vacations
Teachers	Christmas
Food	Fears
Grandparents	Jobs
School	Failures

Finally, remember that your message starts and finishes with Jesus. Read what happened when Peter and John preached one of their first sermons: "When [the members of the Sanhedrin] saw the courage of Peter and John and realized that they were unschooled, ordinary men, they were astonished and they took note that these men had been with Jesus" (Acts 4:13, NIV).

Dr. Marv Penner is Director of the Canadian Center for Adolescent Research and the chairman of the Youth and Family Ministry Department, Briercrest College and Seminary, Caronport, Saskatchewan. He is the author of *Creative Bible Lessons in 1 & 2 Corinthians* and *Youth Worker's Guide to Parenting Ministry*.

Drew Dyson

*is the associate pastor at
Clinton United Methodist Church
in Clinton, New Jersey. He has
worked with youth for ten years and
looks forward to working with youth
for another ten.*

Michael Baughman

*recently earned his Master of Divinity and
Master of Arts in youth ministry degrees
from Princeton Theological Seminary.*

*These guys are great communicators. They
know how to talk about difficult faith
concepts in language that youth understand
and appreciate. They have contributed to
this book a "best of" collection from their
talks. You can just run these talks through
your personal filter and use them almost
as they are. The writers have noted
where you will need to use your own
illustrations. But some of their
illustrations are great, so you
might want to say, "I heard this
story from a friend."*

1. Understanding Salvation

Key Points

Salvation

The Point: to help youth understand the depth of God's love for them by explaining salvation using an illustration. Become familiar with the text because you will be drawing as you speak.

① Was God pleased with Jesus?

How do we know this? Mark 1:9-11

The Scripture: "In those days Jesus came from Nazareth of Galilee and was baptized by John in the Jordan. And just as he was coming up out of the water, he saw the heavens torn apart and the Spirit descending like a dove on him. And a voice came from heaven, 'You are my Son, the Beloved; with you I am well pleased.' ... Then Jesus gave a loud cry and breathed his last. And the curtain of the temple was torn in two, from top to bottom" (Mark 1:9-11; 15:37-38).

Luke 23:39-43 (Salvation) 2 choices
✝ ✝ ✝

Start Talking

[Tell a funny story about a time when what you had planned didn't happen and, while what did happen was not intended, the situation turned out better than you had originally expected.]

Speak the Word

🖰 This is the way it was—the way it is supposed to be.

[Draw a long rectangle and write "God" and "us" in the box.]

🖰

> **God**   **Us**

We wandered in the garden of life with God. We were not God and God was not us, but we were truly together. But something happened—human beings defied God's law. We broke the relationship between us and God, and in so doing a wall of separation was formed between us.

[Draw a thick wall between "God" and "us" With the words "sin" and "death" on it.]

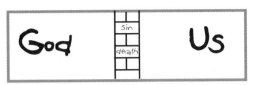

We are separated from God by this overwhelming wall of sin.

[Darken the wall between "God" and "us" with your marker.]

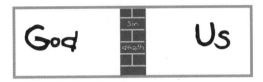

What in the world today shows our separation from God?

[Listen for answers such as "feelings of emptiness," "suffering," or "an inability to solve world problems such as hunger."]

Crowd Participation Idea

Have a volunteer come up and try to get a rock to jump up in the air by yelling at it.

Hear the bad news: None of us have the power to break down this wall. In fact, this wall is so great that some people don't realize that anything is on the other side. We are as powerless to tear down this wall as a rock is to jump into the air when we yell at it. The rock cannot move on its own and neither can we break down this wall. In fact, we even thicken this wall.

Does anyone know how or why we continue to build up this wall?

[Some youth will probably shout out "sin!" If time permits, draw bricks on the wall and ask the youth to "lay the bricks" by naming some of the sins we commit. Write these sins on the individual bricks.]

Hear the good news: God doesn't like this wall. Immediately after this wall was formed, God began breaking it down.

[Draw a few crooked lines through the wall.]

God spoke through the wall to Cain, Noah, Abraham, Moses, David, Solomon, and all the prophets.

⚘ Hear some more good news. God doesn't like this wall and God has the power to take it down. [**Read aloud Mark 1:9-11.**] What happened to the heavens? They were "torn apart." The wall between the earth and the heavens was torn at Jesus' baptism.

[Redraw the rectangle, "God," and "us." This time, draw a wall with a narrow, jagged passage going from one side to the other.]

The wall has been broken. Look at what happens.

[Draw a line moving from the "God side" to the "us side."]

Now God has access to us. Through the birth of Jesus and through the penetrating power of the Holy Spirit, God has access to us! Before we do anything at all, the grace of God has already broken into this world. The wall isn't as much of a barrier as some might think.

What have you seen or experienced in the world that suggests that there isn't a complete separation between us and God?

[Listen for answers such as, "The fact that people show up to church suggests that people long for God"; "The fact that people want to do good things for one another suggests that people are listening to God"; or, "The fact that we even believe in God suggests that the wall has been broken."]

So are all our problems solved? Well, not really. You see in this picture that God has access to us, but the relationship isn't complete. We don't have the ability to get to God. The break in the wall is too small and we keep laying brick upon brick of our own sin. Our sin is always trying to patch up the hole created by the birth of Christ and work of the Holy Spirit. But God is tenacious and will not let that happen. God has done two things: The first is the cross.

[Draw the cross on God's side of the wall.]

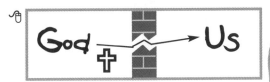

Read aloud Mark 15:37-38.

This is what happens at the moment of Jesus' death. The room that the temple curtain sectioned off was the "holy of holies." According to first century Judaism, God dwelt in that space and the whole surrounding world was the land of "us." It is no coincidence that the curtain that separated "God's room" from the rest of the world was torn in two when Jesus died on the cross! Jesus died, and Jesus felt separated from God. On the cross, the one who was without sin—God's own son— paid the price of sin. This is pretty heavy stuff. The cross broke down the wall in incredible ways.

[Draw a big arrow from the cross toward the wall.]

And the wall—built with the bricks of our sin—is cleared so that we might have newfound closeness to God.

Movie Idea

Show the clip from *American Beauty* where Ricky Fitz shows his girl-friend the video he shot of a plastic bag dancing in the wind. End the clip after he says "and my heart is just gonna' cave in," (Make sure you review the clip first).

Connection: God blesses us with brief moments of beauty when we experience what the other side of the wall is like. Such a moment could happen on a retreat or during a service project. It may happen while watching a sunrise, receiving Communion, or watching a plastic bag dance in the wind. A "moment" may last fifteen minutes or fifteen seconds, but in the kingdom of God it will last fifteen eternities. When we die, we can cross the cross into the other side and experience God's presence eternally.

See the note on video licensing on page 175.

[Draw the picture again with only pieces of the wall remaining. Make sure the edges of the pieces are jagged to show the messy nature of God's destruction of the wall.]

What has happened to death and sin? Like a powerful battering ram, the cross has taken down the wall of sin and death. Through the cross we are forgiven of our sins and through the cross we are able to enter the kingdom of heaven.

[Draw an arrow from "us" to "God" that goes over the cross.

Wrap It Up

Let's recap. Look over the pictures and name some of the important aspects of salvation.

[Encourage answers such as: "We started out in and are supposed to be in an intimate relationship with God"; "We are separated from God by sin and death"; "We can do nothing to break down the wall of sin and death"; "God breaks through the wall because God wants to be with us"; "No part of our world is not touched by God"; "God destroys the wall of sin and death through the cross"; "Because of what God has done, we can not only experience God on earth but also can follow the cross into God's heavenly kingdom."]

What is this kingdom like? What is it like in God's room? We can only imagine the glory that we will find. Because God's kingdom is different from our world it is hard to know. Every now and then, however, we get a glimpse, a thin glimpse of what it might be like.

So What?

- If someone were to ask you about salvation, what would you need to know in order to answer the question? What would you say?
- If God does all the work in breaking down the wall between us and God, what is our role in salvation?
- Have you ever been given a glimpse of the God's kingdom? Can you describe it? What did you feel?
- How are we to live differently because we are saved?
- What do you think heaven is like?

Worship Idea

Play on CD or have your youth band play "Breathing" by Lifehouse or "I Can Only Imagine" by mercyme. Invite your youth to think about what salvation means to them. Encourage them to pray that salvation won't just be an abstract concept for them, but that they will live transformed lives because of what Christ did for them.

Speaker's Note

This talk is meant to convey basic points of salvation upon which most churches can agree. Depending on your church's theology, you may need to adapt the "wall of separation" model and message. If you are not sure about your church's theology of salvation, you might want to meet with your church's senior pastor so that she or he might help you customize this sermon for your tradition.

2. Understanding Sin

The Point: to help youth understand sin and why we needed to be saved from it

The Scripture: "For I know my transgressions, and my sin is ever before me. Against you, you alone, have I sinned, and done what is evil in your sight" (Psalm 51:3-4a).

Movie Idea

Show the clip of *The Lion King* in which the hyenas are dancing around mocking Mufasa's name. See the note on permissions on page 175.

Note: Your youth will probably remember this scene, so play with it for a minute. Let them say, "Mufasa," then shudder.

Start Talking

Does anyone here remember seeing *The Lion King* for the first time? I remember the first time I saw that movie. I was with a group of my friends. One line from the movie became part of our regular speech for weeks. The line came from the three hyenas—Shinzi, Ed, and Banzai—when they were talking about their fear of Mufasa, the king of the jungle. Every time one of them would say his name, Mufasa, all three would shudder. Like this: "Mufasa" (shudder). "Mufasa" (shudder). Then they started laughing uncontrollably.

Every time sin is mentioned in church, it evokes the same reaction. "Sin" (shudder). "Sin" (shudder). Something about the word "sin" makes us uncomfortable. Just knowing that I will be talking about sin is probably making some of you nervous. [Call out to some of the youth: "I can see the fear on your face, Maggie" or "I can see you wiggling in your seat, Will."] Sin makes us so uncomfortable because we can all identify with it. Like Paul said, "All have sinned and fall short of the glory of God" (Romans 3:23).

Speak the Word

Well, for the next few minutes we're going to talk about sin (shudder). Specifically, let's talk about the difference between "little *s*" sins and "Big *S*" sin. No, I'm not saying that some sins are bigger than others. We're not going to use a rating system to determine what qualifies as "Big *S*" sin. I'm talking about the difference between transgressions ("little *s*" sins) and the human condition of sin ("Big *S*" Sin).

🖑 "Little *s*" sins are those willful acts that we do (or don't do) that violate God's law.

Note

If you are not using the presentation on the CD–Rom, write "little *s*" and "Big *S*" on a markerboard or large sheet of paper.

What are some examples of "little *s*" sins that you experience everyday? [Write their answers on the markerboard or large sheet of paper. For example: lying, cheating, cursing, and so on.]

Most of these sins are things that human beings do to other human beings that violate the law and will of God. But sins can also be things that humans *don't* do for others.

What are some "little *s*" sins that are things people *don't* do but should? [Write their answers on the markerboard or large sheet of paper. For example: not feeding the hungry, being silent when an offensive joke is told, and so on.]

The Bible is full of accounts of people committing "little *s*" sins. Think of David, in a fit of lust, having sex with another man's wife. Or Moses, in a fit of rage, killing an Egyptian. Think of Cain killing his brother Abel, or Achan's attempt to hide his disobedience from God and the people of Israel. Think of Peter's denial of Jesus or Paul's persecution of Christians. And the story of "little *s*" sins continues throughout history.

Some people take people from other nations and force them into slavery. Some people build concentration camps to attempt to rid the world of an "inferior" religion or ethnic group. Some people fly planes into buildings or strap bombs to themselves to blow up buses. And the story continues today.

Some people lie in order to make themselves look better. Some people cheat on tests because they didn't take the time to study. Some people tell jokes and make remarks that dehumanize others. These actions, or lack of action, are "little *s*" sins that cause people like you and me to act contrary to God's will for our lives. But these sins are only a symptom of a greater problem.

While "little *s*" sins are easier to identify, "Big *S*" sin is the heart of the problem. 🖑 "Big *S*" sin is the human condition shared by all people. It is alienation and separation from the holy, living

God. Adam and Eve's story tells us something fundamental about who we are: When they ate the fruit from the tree of the knowledge of good and evil, sin entered the world. Human beings, who once enjoyed the pleasure of God's constant presence, were now aware of their sin and separated from God. The condition of sin, or "Big *S*" sin, causes us to act against God's will.

Read aloud Psalm 51:3-4a.

The psalmist is aware of this condition. He writes about knowing his sin all of the time. This problem of sin isn't new to us. Way back when this psalm was written, people struggled with sin.

Isn't it great to watch children play in the snow? They can spend hours making snow angels, building forts, and hurling snowballs. But, the ultimate snow day event is building a snowman. Most children put all of their creativity into this endeavor and usually find great ways to make their snowmen unique. The only problem is that, without fail, every time a child builds a snowman, it melts and that child is crushed. Five-year-olds just can't understand that a snowman melts because of what it is made of. In the same way, humans commit sins ("little *s*"), because of what we are made of: We share the inheritance of the condition of sin ("Big *S*").

Wrap It Up

But the story doesn't end there. The good news of God's amazing love is that we are never without the grace of God. John Wesley said, "No [human] is wholly void of the grace of God." Paul said: The amazing thing is this: "While we were still sinners Christ died for us" (Romans 5:8). All humans share the condition of sin. But, all humans also share in God's grace. God loved us so much to send Jesus Christ to die for us. God has been drawing us closer since long before any of us was even aware of it.

Maybe the reason the word *sin* causes people to shudder is that they don't know the full story. Without the love of God in Jesus Christ, we would have reason to be afraid. But because of God's amazing love and grace, the only word that should make us shudder is ... "Mufasa" (shudder).

So What?

- How can we overcome the desire to sin?
- What is God saying to you now about your sin?

3. Experiencing Forgiveness

The Point: to help youth understand the depth of forgiveness Christ offers to them

The Scripture: "But God, who is rich in mercy, out of the great love with which he loved us even when we were dead through our trespasses, made us alive together with Christ" (Ephesians 2:4-5a).

Start Talking

Are there any romantics here today? I'm a romantic. [If you are a romantic, tell a story about your own experience. If not, you might want to illustrate with a movie clip or song.]

Speak the Word

Maybe she was a romantic too:

She made one mistake at sixteen years old and now she was paying for it, for sure. She allowed herself to fall in love. Believed that he, at twenty-three, loved her too. Her father didn't love her—he left when she was ten. Her mother worked and never paid attention to her. But *he* treated her like a princess. Finally, she was loved. *Until*, they were caught. Now she was dragged from his bed and brought to the temple. Thrown onto the floor in disgust in front of the one they call Jesus. The crowd circled around her shouting loudly and angrily. She looked up saw him, the one she loved, in the crowd with a stone in his

Story Idea

(Here's my story. You might have an even funnier one!)

At age six I was engaged several times. I would write on "first grade" paper (the kind with only three big lines on each page):

Dear Susan,
Will you marry me?
___ Yes or ___ No
Love,
Me

My success rate was pretty high for a first grader. When my wife and I got married, I had to confess that I had been engaged eleven times before. By age eleven I was writing love songs and poems. Here's one of my best:

In all my life,
I have met only one
who has parted the clouds
and brought the sun.
Your beautiful smile
warms my heart;
I'm so full of love,
I've got to fart!

That's good stuff for an eleven-year-old!

My Story

When I was 8 years old, I broke *the* pitcher. You know the one that your mother protects with all of her life and hides during every family gathering. I decided that I needed to practice my baseball swing in the house. Before I could "check my swing," I hit the table that held "the pitcher." In slow motion, the pitcher fell to the ground as I dove in a feeble attempt save it.

My brother saw the whole thing and, in a way that only older brothers can, said: "I'm telling … UNLESS you become my servant." For 6 days, I did everything he asked of me. I made his bed. I cleaned his room. I washed his feet. Finally, I couldn't take it anymore, and I went to my mom to confess. Before I could finish, she said: "I knew the day it happened and I forgave you then. I was testing how long you'd let your brother be the boss."

hand. But then the teacher bent down and wrote in the sand. And the crowd grew silent. "Let any one of you who is without sin throw the first stone." He bent down and wrote some more. When he looked up again, the crowd was gone. He turned to her, cupped her face in his hands, and set her free: free from her mistakes, free from her past, free from her sin.

Do you ever wonder what Jesus wrote in the sand?

Maybe he wrote Scripture. Maybe he listed sins. Maybe he wrote names. Maybe he wrote the name of the man the woman loved. Whatever he wrote, the religious accusers, who stood ready to stone the woman, disappeared. This story has much to say to those who stand in judgment over the "sinners" of our day. But today we will focus on three stops on the journey of forgiveness.

⁀ The first stop on the road is *receiving* God's forgiveness. All of us in this room cover up some part of us—some blemish we want to hide, some part of ourselves that we'd rather not share. Paul says that we all sin and fall short of God's glory. In order to follow Jesus, we need to receive the forgiveness that he offers. Here's the good news: We can't earn it and don't deserve it.

Many of us are held captive by our pasts. We allow our sins to keep us from receiving all that God has in store for us. The good news is that our heavenly parent has already witnessed everything we've done and said, "I love you anyway."

Read aloud Ephesians 2:4-5.

⁀ God loves us unconditionally and forgives us no matter what we have done. The problem is that many of us never open

Scripture Talks: 50 Creative Messages for Youth

ourselves up to receive that forgiveness.

Jesus *set* the woman free. She became aware of her sin and was assured that Christ forgave her. But she was *sent* free with a command, a choice of whether she would receive that forgiveness: "Go your way, and from now on do not sin again" (John 8:11b).

Maybe some of you have never allowed Christ to cleanse you and make you whole, to set you free from the sin that entangles you, and to receive God's gift of eternal life. Like the adulterous woman, you will leave here with a choice. ✝ How will you answer?

✝ The second stop on the road of forgiveness is forgiving yourself. This is often the hardest stop on the road.

The second stop is usually where Christians get stuck. We have decided to allow Christ to come in and cleanse our sin. We have received the gift of eternal life. Yet we still fall into the trap of deeming ourselves unworthy. We allow our sin to stake claim on our lives and we refuse to let it go . . . even if God has forgiven us.

Forgiving yourself means not allowing faults and failures of the past to determine how you look at yourself now. ✝ You are a child of God, set free by grace. You worthy and loveable. You are free.

✝ The final stop on this road is forgiving others. I wonder if Jesus' words to the woman, "Go your way, and from now on, do not sin again," were a reminder for her to forgive the very people who dragged her out to stone her in the first place. They had dragged her from bed. They had let the man who was with her go. They held rocks above their heads and foamed at the mouth, ready to hurl them at her and end her life. And Jesus asked her, "Where are they? Has no one condemned you? . . . Go your way, and from now on, do not sin again" (John 8:10b, 11b).

My Story

Rachel wept every time she came up for Holy Communion. After several weeks, I finally got up the courage to ask what was bothering her. She responded, "It reminds me of how many people that I've hurt." Rachel had run away from her family, fallen into a life of drugs, and finally come home because she was too sick to survive on her own anymore. As a Christian, she had received God's forgiveness, and she had reconciled with her family, but she had not forgiven herself.

"Just as I have forgiven you, you ought to forgive those who brought you here." That is why we pray in the Lord's prayer, "forgive us our sins as we forgive those who sin against us." ◦

As forgiven people, we are called to forgive others.

Closing

Close this sermon with a personal story about your own experience of forgiveness. If you have trouble thinking of a story, you might turn to contemporary stories of forgiveness by Christian authors, such as Max Lucado or Philip Yancey. Regardless, end with an invitation for young people to be forgiven and to forgive.

Wrap It Up

Some of us here are holding on to a hurt and need to forgive someone in our lives. You may have seen your parents' marriage fall apart or one of your friends may have broken a promise. God calls us to let go of the pain that holds us and to forgive those who have hurt us. Forgiving others doesn't guarantee that the hurt will go away, but it does means that you have the power to let it go on your end.

The journey of forgiveness is not an easy road, but is one that we all must travel if we are to follow Christ.

So What? ◦

◦ What does it mean to receive God's forgiveness?
◦ How have you experienced forgiveness in your life?
◦ To whom have you offered forgiveness? To whom do you need to offer forgiveness?

4. Getting a Grip on Grace

The Point: to help youth see God's grace at work

The Scripture: "The Spirit helps us in our weakness; for we do not know how to pray as we ought, but that very Spirit intercedes . . . . For those whom he foreknew he also predestined to be conformed to the image of his Son . . . . And those whom he predestined he also called; and those whom he called he also justified; and those whom he justified he also glorified" (Romans 8:26-30).

Start Talking

"P" can mean a lot of things. It's the sixteenth letter of the alphabet. It's the first letter of words like pickle, pear, and petunia. "P" can also mean a vegetable—those tiny green balls of mush that find their way to our plates every so often. They don't have much taste, but their texture is pretty disgusting. Of course, "p" can also refer to a routine bodily function.

Speak the Word

Today, I want to emphasize the letter "p" as we talk about God's grace. ⏎ Grace is unearned, undeserved favor from God. Grace is God giving us the best when we deserve the worst. God's grace works in our lives in different ways.

Story idea

(Here's my story. Use it or one of your own.)

A few years ago I was returning to New Jersey with a group of high school students I had taken to a Habitat for Humanity service project. Before we left the church in Virginia, where we had stayed, I gave the obligatory instruction: "Go to the bathroom now because we will not stop for at least two hours." Needless to say, 45 minutes into the trip someone in one of the trailing cars had to stop. But I wouldn't be deterred. I drove ahead avoiding the flashing lights and high beams. Finally, the car made its way alongside me and the adult in the passenger's seat made a pleading face and held up a sign. Guess what it had on it? The letter "p". From that day on, the letter "p" had a whole new place in our youth group's lore.

A helpful way to get a grip on grace comes from eighteenth-century church father John Wesley. He understood grace to have

My Story

For me grace is the consistent love of Christians who continually told me of God's incredible love for me—even at times when I felt that no one could love me. Growing up, I was around "church stuff" all the time. But it wasn't a sermon or a program or a campfire that brought me to accept Christ as my personal savior. It was the unbelievable knowledge that God loved me simply for who I was.

When I look back on the people God used to nudge me into a relationship, I see an endless array of teachers, youth leaders, prayer warriors, and especially my mother. I remember that during a particularly rebellious time of my life (try and control your shock), I came home from a party several hours past my curfew. Rather than finding the fight that I was waiting for, I found a note on my bed that read: "I love you and so does God. I'm praying for you. Sleep well!" I was ticked! This letter drove me crazy! But, it led me to think about the path that I was going down and pointed me in a new direction.

three different forms or three distinct ways of working in someone's life: The "three p's" of grace.

First is the *prodding* grace of God. Prodding grace works in our lives before we are even aware of God's presence. It is God knowing our name and calling us, trying to get our attention. It is God working in our lives to draw us.

That's the prodding of God's grace. Before we are even aware of it, God is working in our lives poking and prodding us toward God. Can you feel that grace in your own life or identify how it has touched you in your past? Maybe it was through a schoolteacher or a friend. Maybe through the words of your parents or prayers of your grandparents. God's incredible gift of love gently calls us and prods us towards a relationship with God.

Next is the *pardoning* grace of God. This is God's act of grace that makes it all real. God calls our name and continually prods us into a relationship. Then, through that relationship, God offers us forgiveness. We accept that love and forgiveness and our lives are changed. In that moment we surrender our lives to God and Jesus becomes our friend, our Savior, our Lord; he becomes our lifeline, not just a name.

We all stand in need of God's forgiveness. The pardoning grace of God (or, as Wesley called it, "justifying" grace) brings us into a right relationship with God. Through Christ's death on the cross on our behalf, we can stand before God with a clean slate. Think of it this way: just-i-fied—"just-if-I'd" never sinned.

Scripture Talks: 50 Creative Messages for Youth

Another way to look at pardoning grace is to think of 'new birth.' Some of you may know the story of Roy Riegels: On New Year's Day, 1929, Georgia Tech played UCLA in the Rose Bowl. In that game, a young man named Roy Riegels recovered a fumble for UCLA. In the scramble for the loose ball, he lost his direction and ran 65 yards toward the wrong goal line. One of his teammates ran him down and tackled him just before he scored for the opposing team. Several plays later, UCLA was forced to punt. Tech blocked the kick and scored a safety, demoralizing UCLA just before the half.

My Story

When I was seven years old, I used to go to my father's office at his church and put on his robe and a stole. I would stand in the pulpit and preach to the empty pews. I wanted to be just like daddy! I must have looked pretty ridiculous to everyone but my father. He remembers the hours we spent together playing church and he never commented on how ridiculous I looked in his robe.

During halftime, Roy put a blanket on his shoulders, sat down in a corner and put his face in his hands. His coach, who usually had a lot to say during halftime, was quiet. The coach was obviously trying to decide what to do with Roy. Just before the second half, the coach finally spoke. He said simply, "Men, the same team that played the first half will start the second."

The players got up and started out. But Roy didn't budge. The coach called him again and he still didn't move. Finally the coach went over to Roy and said, "Roy, didn't you hear me? The same team that played in the first half will start the second!" Roy, his cheeks wet with tears, looked at his coach and said, "Coach, I can't do it. I've ruined you. I've ruined the university's reputation. I've ruined myself. There's no way I can face that crowd." The coach put his hand on Roy's shoulder and said, "Roy, get up and get out there. The game is only half over." He finally got up, went onto the field, and played an inspired second half of football.

All of us have run in the wrong direction at some point. Some of us here might still be running in that direction. The good news is that, because of God's pardoning grace, the game is only half over. The prodding love of God whispers to us that we are loved and the pardoning grace of God gives us a second chance.

✝ Once we have accepted God's pardoning grace, God's *perfecting* grace takes over, leading us into a life that each and every day becomes more and more like the life of Jesus. Wesley called this grace "sanctifying" grace.

We are similar to seven-year-olds in the pulpit when we come before Jesus. We want to be as loving and kind and caring as Jesus is. We want to emulate his compassion and his forgiveness. We want our lives to make a difference just like his did. And the good news is that, through the Holy Spirit and the continuing grace of God, we can become more and more like Christ! While we now may seem like seven-year-olds in preachers' robes, God's perfecting grace can help us reach our dream of being just like daddy!

Wrap It Up

God's perfecting grace is at work in our lives when we open ourselves to be the hands and feet of Jesus in the world, when we offer ourselves in love to our neighbor, and when we stand for justice and work for peace. God's perfecting grace continues to mold us throughout our lives so that every day, in small and large ways, we are becoming more and more like Jesus Christ.

So What?

- How have you experienced God's prodding grace?
- How have you reacted to experiencing God's pardoning grace?
- How is God's grace at work in you now, perfecting and molding you to be more like Christ?

5. Experiencing Communion

The Point: to help youth understand Holy Communion and experience it more fully

The Scripture: "For as often as you eat this bread and drink the cup, you proclaim the Lord's death until he comes" (1 Corinthians 11:26).

Start Talking

[Bring out a plate of Spam® and hold it up for your youth. Use a fork and take a bite for effect. Before or after your talk you may also want to have a "Spam®-eating contest."]

⊕ How many of you have ever eaten "mystery meat"? You know what I'm talking about. They probably serve it every Wednesday at school. When I was in high school, there was something appealing about the mystery meat. Even though we had no idea what it was, we still ate it. Something about it kept me coming back every Wednesday at 11:05 A.M.

Like students who are unsure about the meat on their cafeteria trays, many Christians, when taking Communion, think "I don't necessarily know what this is, but I know it must be good for me." It's a holy meal with a bit of mystery. So what is this holy meal?

Speak the Word

First, the celebration of Holy Communion, or Eucharist, is a holy meal of remembrance. ⊕ By taking Communion, we remember.

Every time we gather around the communion table we remember Jesus Christ in life—the joy that he shared and the way that he taught us to live lives of love for God and others. We also remember Jesus Christ in death and the love that he poured out for us in his blood when he died on the cross. And we remember Christ's resurrection: the ultimate pronouncement that, because he has conquered death, so can we!

Holy Communion is also a celebration of Christ's presence with us through the struggles of our life. Just as we remember what God has done through Jesus Christ in the past, we celebrate that Christ continues to act in and through our lives in the present. Communion is the reassurance that Jesus Christ travels with us on the journey of life.

In the book *Sleeping With Bread*, Dennis, Sheila, and Matthew Linn tell the story of the thousands of children who were orphaned during the bombing raids of World War II. The fortunate ones were rescued and placed in refugee camps where they received food and good care. But many of the children in these camps couldn't sleep at night. They feared waking up and finding themselves homeless again and without food. Nothing seemed to assure them until a nun in charge of one of the camps came up with an idea. Immediately before bedtime, each child would receive a piece of bread to hold while he or she slept. Holding tightly to their bread, the children could finally sleep in peace. All through the night the bread reminded them: Today we ate and tomorrow we will eat again.

[Move to the Communion table.] The bread that we eat now is bread for our journey, bread that will sustain us throughout every difficulty, bread that will nourish us when nothing else will.

The bread is Jesus' presence with us and a sacrament that transforms us. But Communion carries with it some responsibility. A famous theologian named John Howard Yoder states that in receiving this holy meal, we are bound to a different way of living—a way of living where peace outlives war, love outdoes hatred, and sacrificial giving to the poor and needy outshines the accumulation of wealth and power.

That's why we say in our Communion service: "Make [the bread and wine] be for us the body and blood of Christ *so that* we may be for the world the body of Christ, redeemed by His blood."* [Note: Your tradition may express this sentiment using different words. Use the words that best will help the youth connect the sacred meal with our responsibility in the world.]

* From "A Service of Word and Table I," *The United Methodist Hymnal* (The United Methodist Publishing House, 1993), page 10.

✌ Thirdly, Holy Communion is a meal that reminds us of our hope for the future. Because of the life, death, and resurrection of Jesus Christ, Christian people live with the assurance that God is near. In spite of what is going on in the present, we can be assured that we have hope through Jesus Christ!

As wars rage on around the world; children die daily from starvation; and violence tears apart schools, families, and cities; we can celebrate because, by partaking of this bread and this cup, we claim ultimate victory in Jesus Christ! And in our celebration, we give thanks. Another word for "Communion" is "Eucharist," which literally translated means "to give thanks." In this holy meal, we pause to give thanks for all of the gifts that God has given to us, particularly the gift of Jesus Christ.

Communion is a celebration of remembrance, an assurance of Christ's presence in our lives, and a proclamation that we live in hope because of the life, death, and resurrection of Jesus Christ!

However, in addition to all of these explanations, Communion is still essentially a mystery.

Wrap It Up

Despite the best efforts of clergy and theologians to explain it, the Communion meal is still a mystery. And it is the mystery that draws us back time and time again. In this bread [hold up bread] and in this cup [hold up cup] is Jesus Christ. The bread reminds us of Jesus' body, which, in living and in dying, taught us to love. The cup, the blood of salvation, reminds us of Jesus Christ's radical sacrifice on the cross—the pain, the agony, and the separation from God that Jesus experienced.

In Communion we taste and see that the Lord is good! We experience God in the most literal sense. Jesus enters our bodies and we carry his love into the world that we are called to serve!

So What?

- What special "remembrances" does your family observe?
- What is your most memorable Communion experience?
- How do you feel when you talk or think about the "body" and "blood" of Jesus Christ?
- What do you think about, pray for, or reflect on when you take Communion?

Worship Idea

Invite a member of your pastoral staff or other ordained clergy to lead your group in Holy Communion. Have your band or song leader lead the group in some prayer songs and then spend some time in silence thinking about the mystery of Christ's real presence with us.

6. Baptism

The Point: to help youth understand what it means to live as baptized Christians

The Scripture: "I have baptized you with water; but he will baptize you with the Holy Spirit" (Mark 1:8).

Start Talking

🕯 Baptism begins with water. No matter what church you belong to, no matter where you are born, and no matter how you are baptized, baptism begins with water. As we try to understand baptism, let's talk about water for a minute.

[Ask the youth to name the properties of water and to describe what water is like and what it can do. Record these answers on a markerboard or large sheet of paper and reference these answers throughout your talk.]

Today I want to help us understand baptism a little better by thinking about the water. Water is required for living. It restores dying things and sustains life. Water is refreshing and cooling.

Note

If you want to add a little excitement (and if you are not giving this talk in the middle of a Minnesota winter), pull out a high-powered water gun and randomly spray kids with it to "remind them what water is like."

Speak the Word

Baptism is about death and life. One of our most important beliefs about our baptism is that through baptism we die to ourselves and rise from the waters into a new creation. We believe that, when we are covered by the baptismal waters, our lives as independent individuals end and our lives in the body of Christ begin. As baptized Christians, we no longer live for ourselves, but for God and the church.

Baptism is not just about dying, though. We have to remember that water is also necessary for life. Did you know that if all the water were removed from a 150 pound person, that person would then weigh about 50 pounds? A human being can go three weeks without food, but going three days without water is deadly. Just as we need water to sustain our lives, we also need Living Water to sustain our souls. ✛ In baptism we die to ourselves and allow the Living Water to live in us.

So what does it mean to live a baptized life? Well first, a baptized person finds him- or herself connected to the body of Christ. To help us understand this connection, we're going to make rain.

[Make "rain" in a space that fits your youth group. If the space is too open, the sound and effect gets lost.]

To make rain we will first rub our hands together. [Demonstrate by rubbing your hands together.] Then we'll snap our fingers. [Demonstrate by snapping with both hands, alternating hands.] Next, we'll move on to patting our laps. [Demonstrate by patting your lap, again alternating hands.] Then we'll stomp our feet. [Demonstrate by stomping your feet, alternating feet.] Finally, we'll work backwards by patting our lap, then snapping, and then rubbing our hands. Follow my lead so that you will know when to switch. [Turn out or dim the lights to add to the effect. Do each of the actions (rubbing your hands, snapping your fingers, patting your lap, and stomping) for twenty seconds each in the order indicated below.]

Rubbing ⟶ Snapping ⟶ Patting ⟶ Stomping ⟶
Patting ⟶ Snapping ⟶ Rubbing ⟶ Silence

Debrief this experience by asking:

- Did our movements sound like rain?
- What if only one of us had done the motions? Would it have sounded like rain?

This is one of the most important truths of baptism: We don't *just* die to ourselves; we don't *just* find new life in the Spirit; but we are born into a mighty and powerful community that can accomplish things as a group that no individual could accomplish by him- or herself. ✛ The baptized community can change the landscape of society as a massive tidal wave that washes away injustice or as a trickling river that slowly wears away the opposition of rocky sin.

[Refer to anything the youth may have said earlier about the abundance of water in the world.] Just as water can cover the earth, the waters of baptism entirely cover our lives. When we are baptized—whether we're sprinkled, dunked, or spritzed—every part of us is covered by God's grace and filled with the Holy Spirit. Hands are washed with grace to do God's work. Feet are washed with grace to go where God leads. Mouths are washed with grace to preach God's word. Ears are washed with grace to better hear the word of God. Every part of us is covered in God's grace!

֎ Our souls are washed clean. By dying in the water of our baptism and being raised again into new life in the community, the stain of sin is removed. We are washed clean. And, whether we are baptized at ninety-four years or four days old, we are God's beloved children.

Wrap It Up

Are you ready to make rain? Are you ready to rain down justice that will cover the earth like mighty waters? Are you ready to rain down righteousness that will flow through the world like a stream? Are you ready to make it rain and change your school? Are you ready to make it rain in your family, in your church, in your town, in the world? Are you ready to make it rain?

God has the power to make it rain through you. Sure we can make it sound like rain, but true rain comes only from the "reign" of God. If you want to experience rain and want to be a part of God's rain, I ask you:

Are you ready to give in to the reign of God that gives new life? Are you ready to be covered by the reign of grace that washes over all that you are and all that you will be? ֎ Are you ready to be soaked by the divine downpour of love that covers the earth? If you are, then you just might be ready to share some of that rain with others. [Liven up the conclusion by pausing, then busting out the high-powered water gun and having a little fun.]

So What? ֎

- If baptism means dying to yourself and living a new life in Christ, what does baptism mean for everyday living?
- What role does God play in your baptism?

7. Service or Servanthood?

Note

This sermon begins with a meditation. To familiarize yourself with the text, practice reading it aloud prior to giving your talk. Ask all of the youth to close their eyes and imagine themselves in the following situation. Allow some time for nervous giggles. Once the giggles have died down, begin the meditation.

The Point: to empower youth to model Christ by living a life of servanthood

The Scripture: "Christ Jesus, who, though he was in the form of God, did not regard equality with God as something to be exploited, but emptied himself, taking the form of a slave, being born into human likeness. And being found in human form, he humbled himself and became obedient to the point of death" (Philippians 2:5a-8).

Start Talking

You're standing on the service side of a soup kitchen line. What do you feel? [Pause.] Maybe you feel the crinkling gloves that loosely fit around your fingers or the heat from the buffet tray. Maybe you feel an emptiness in your stomach—you've been cooking all morning but have not yet had the chance to eat. [Pause.]

What do you smell? [Pause.] Do you smell the green beans from the tray in front of you or the vegetable soup in the large pot next to you? Does the sharp smell of hot dogs at 10:30 in the morning make you uneasy? Maybe you notice the smell of some persons who have not had the chance to bathe recently. [Pause.]

The green beans are heavy on your spoon as you carefully fill the appropriate section of a man's plate. "Enjoy," you say with a smile. He nods and moves on—he is thankful for the food, but his enthusiasm does not match yours. As you place green beans on the next man's plate, you smile again and encourage him to enjoy. He responds with a quick "thank you" then shuffles on to the soup. You serve at least fifty people and although a few give you a sincere and hearty "thank you," most never even look up to see your smile. You want them to know that you love them, but they don't seem to notice or care.

Invite your group to open their eyes.

Speak the Word

In the scenario you just envisioned, you were providing a service. People were hungry and you served them food. ⚘ We are called to *service* as Christians. But we're also called to *servanthood*. In servanthood we take service one step further by forming relationships with those whom we serve. How could you have expressed servanthood in the scenario?

[Some may respond: "By asking the persons about their day." Press them to go deeper. Hopefully at least one youth will think of sitting down and eating with persons being served.]

When you take the time to sit down and talk with the people you are serving, you begin to serve as Christ did. How would your relationship with a man or woman who is poor change by sitting down and eating with him or her? [Give youth the chance to respond. Make sure to affirm their answers.]

Relationships among God's creatures have been harmed by distinctions of who is cool and who is not; who is annoying and who is funny; who looks good and who looks plain; whether someone is a girl or a boy, old or young, white or black or yellow or tan. [Feel free to add any distinctions that separate youth in your church or community.]

Sometimes peace seems impossible because feelings have been hurt and nerves have been cut. Relationships can be difficult between persons who are serving and persons who are being served, but if we are to live lives of servanthood, we are called twist the shape of our lives to meet the needs of another.

Did you know that your generation is the generation most likely to perform acts of service? Statistics say that people your age spend more time volunteering than any other generation in history. Many of you practice service, but how many of you practice servanthood. Let's look at some of the distinctions between service and servanthood:

Service is helping other members of the youth group on a service project. ⚘ Servanthood is washing their feet at the end of the day.

Service is getting your friends to stop picking on someone who isn't as cool as you. ✝ Servanthood is sitting with that someone at lunch.

Service is using your skills to build a house for Habitat for Humanity. ✝ Servanthood is teaching someone who is new to construction how to use certain tools or perform certain tasks.

Service is making tea for your parents at the end of the day. ✝ Servanthood is sitting down with them and asking them how their day went.

Service is dropping off your younger sister at a friend's house. ✝ Servanthood is making sure that she is safe before you leave.

Is service bad? NO! We are called to service. We don't always take the time or energy for servanthood. But we should remember that God calls us to go beyond service.

Service is giving out food in a soup kitchen line. Servanthood involves getting out from behind that line and sitting to eat with the people you are serving. How do we know that this is what we are supposed to do? Because this is exactly what God did. It tells us in Philippians 2:5-8 that, ✝ "Christ Jesus, who, though he was in the form of God, did not regard equality with God as something to be exploited, but emptied himself, taking the form of a slave, being born into human likeness. And being found in human form, he humbled himself and became obedient to the point of death." Jesus humbled himself so that we would know God's love.

Wrap It Up

We are called to servanthood because, when we become servants, we show others what God is willing to do for them. We are called to servanthood because becoming servants reminds us of what God has done for us.

The service industry is important to the United States' economy; but you, I, and the church are called to be in the servanthood industry for the good of God's economy. ✝ Servanthood means not looking for thanks, tips, rewards, or titles. Servanthood means looking instead for truth, testimonies, and true relationships of love that reflect the love of Christ.

[Give the following benediction at this point or after allowing time for question and answers or discussion.]

Go from this place, knowing that God has gotten out from behind the buffet line that separates us from the Divine to be with us. Go from this place, knowing that God has asked us to go and do likewise.

So What?

- When has someone become a servant for you? How did this person's servanthood make you feel? Describe the experience to the group if you are comfortable doing so.
- When have you become a servant for someone else? When have you gone beyond service to servanthood? How did it feel to you?
- Why is servanthood harder than service? Who in your life really needs to be touched by your servanthood right now?

8. Fully What?

The Point: to help youth learn to wrestle with theology

The Scripture: "In the beginning was the Word, and the Word was with God, and the Word was God" (John 1:1).

Note

For this message you will need enough markers or crayons so that every youth will have two different colors; one strip of paper for each youth (cut letter-sized sheets of paper into eight strips); and tape.

Start Talking

I think that we in the church often talk about scandalous ideas as if they were nothing. One of the most scandalous and complicated ideas that we talk about a lot is who Jesus is. We're going to spend some time looking at Jesus' mysterious identity.

Speak the Word

Each of you has a strip of paper. I want you to take your strip of paper, twist it once, and tape the two ends together. [See the diagram in the margin.] The structure you've created looks like it has two sides, right? Well, take one of your markers (or crayons) and, starting at one point on one side of the strip, draw a line around the loop until you return to the point where you started. Then take your other marker (or crayon) and do the same thing, but start on the other side of the loop. [If youth have made the strips correctly, both of their lines will follow the same route, covering what appears to be "both sides" of the strip.]

What you have made is called a Mobius Strip. It defies our understanding. No matter how hard we try to distinguish one side from the other, there is only one side. Keep the Mobius strip in mind because it is a stunning metaphor for who Jesus was. More on this in a minute.

We're going to look at some different pictures of Jesus—some of them you may have seen before, others may seem scandalous. We're going to take the time to decide whether each picture is

Mobius Strip

Twist and attach so that *x* touches *x* and *y* touches *y*.

accurate. ✎ [As you show each slide, ask the youth "What do you notice about this picture of Jesus?" and "Is this an accurate picture of Jesus?" Before showing the last slide, say: ✎ "This is by far the most scandalous picture of Jesus, but it is also the most accurate." The last slide is a picture of a baby in the womb. If you are not using the PowerPoint® presentation, show a variety of pictures of Jesus followed by a sonogram photo.]

We cannot know what Jesus looked like. The gospel writers didn't draw any pictures or give us any physical description, but we do know that at some point Jesus looked just like this. God became human for our sake, and that, my friends, makes all the difference.

Jesus is scandalous because Jesus doesn't make sense! When we describe Jesus, we seem to contradict ourselves: Son of God and Son of Man; Messiah and Prince of Peace; fully God and fully human. How can someone be the son of God but be born from humanity? How can the Prince of Peace be the Messiah? How can someone be God and human? Aren't those things supposed to be different?

The short answer is, yes. Although humans are created in God's image, we are completely different from God. It does not make sense for someone to be fully God and fully human. Wouldn't the imperfections of humankind taint the perfect nature of God? Because God is all powerful and perfect, God cannot suffer, but if Jesus was fully divine and fully human, then doesn't that mean that God suffered on the cross? The very existence of Jesus raises a lot of questions, and I think that this is good.

Story Idea

(Here's my story. You may have one just like it. If not, feel free to say that you heard this story from a friend.)

One Sunday, I was giving the pastoral prayer. Early into the prayer, a mother dropped her baby's bottle and said, "oh shoot." But she didn't say "shoot." She was sitting in the front row, though, so I didn't know if anyone else had heard her, until . . .

A group of children sitting near where the bottle incident had occurred clearly heard what the mother had said. I know this because of the resounding chorus of children's voices I heard saying "shoot," "shoot," "shoot," "shoot," "shoot" (giggle, giggle) "shoot."

Only they weren't saying "shoot." I did my best to keep my eyes closed and keep from laughing as I finished the prayer—a task that was complicated by the sound of quiet laughter coming from the senior pastor seated directly behind me.

(*Story Idea continued on page 46.*)

(*Story Idea continued from page 45.*)

While I would normally be a little upset about a chorus of expletives coming from the congregation during a prayer, I was amused by the interchange that occurred. I was amused because not a single child knew what he or she was saying, and it struck me that this often happens in the church. No, I don't think children curse in church all the time, but I do wonder how often we use words in church that we don't understand.

God and how God works in the world defy explanation. Father, Son, Holy Spirit—God is more than we can ever imagine. Like a Mobius strip, some of what we say in the church might look simple, but, when we look really closely, it is bizarre and complex. We can't explain exactly who Jesus was (and is) and what that means for us. This is a challenge for each of us to explore, so that we will really see how scandalous this faith of ours is! The scandal of someone saying the word 'shoot' in church is nothing compared the scandal of saying the Apostles Creed!

Wrap It Up

This faith we profess is not meant be any easier than the life of faith that we are called to live. True discipleship is valuable because it is dirty, messy, uncomfortable, and challenging. True faith is the same way. If you dive in, I promise that you will get dirty, messy and uncomfortable. I also promise that you will love exploring your beliefs for just that reason.

So What?

- What are some other things about God or Christianity that may seem scandalous to the rest of the world?
- If our faith is so scandalous, how should we live it out?
- What else, do you think, do we say in church without realizing its meaning?

9. Take Up Your Mat, and Dance!

The Point: to help youth practice their faith

The Scripture: "Jesus said to him, 'Stand up, take your mat and walk' " (John 5:8).

Start Talking

See the Story Idea

Speak the Word

In Jerusalem there was a pool where the crippled, lame, and blind would go to be healed. According to legend, each day God's spirit came and stirred the waters of the pool, and the first person into the water that day would be healed. So day after day, hundreds of sick people would crowd by the side of the pool waiting to be miraculously healed. One man in particular had been sick for 38 years! And now, every day, he made his way to the poolside hoping and praying for his shot at wholeness.

One day, Jesus walked by, saw this man, and asked him, "Do you want to be made well?" I've struggled with that question for a long time and can't help wondering how I would have reacted to Jesus. I imagine I would have sarcastically replied, "DUH! I've been laying here for years and you come by and ask me if I want to be made well? What do you think I'm doing here? suntanning?!"

Story Idea

(Use this story or one of your own about learning something new.)

It was a ridiculous scene. I was in the middle of a crowded arcade playing *Dance Dance Revolution USA* while five of my junior high youth looked on. A few days earlier I had mentioned to one of them that I couldn't dance. So we made the trek to this teenage mecca. "If you want to learn to dance," my young friend explained, "you've got to start somewhere."

So there I was stomping on a lighted dance floor with all the rhythm and grace of a bull in a china shop. I was stomping, twisting, and sweating to techno-pop dance music while a crowd formed around me. A group of older and wiser senior high youth, much less tactful than their younger peers, were hysterical with laughter.

(*Story Idea continued on page 48.*)

(*Story Idea continued from page 47.*)

Mothers were clinging to their elementary-aged children and giving me disdainful glances. Other adults were simply smirking and giving me the all too familiar "better you than me" look.

And all the while my five junior high students were shouting words of encouragement and instruction.

When it was all over, I labored off the dance floor struggling to catch my breath. As I sat on a bench trying to regain my composure, one of the youth looked at me and said, "Well, you can't dance yet but at least you're on your way." His words immediately made me think of a familiar scene from Scripture.

But, the more I think about it, the more I realize that Jesus' question was not only valid, it was right on the mark. The man's response wasn't a resounding "yes," it was a series of excuses. "I have no one to help me into the water." "Every time the water is stirred, someone else beats me to it." And Jesus, seeing right through his fear, says, "Stand up! Take up your mat, and walk." And the man stands up, takes up his mat, and walks.

Now, if I had been lame for all of that time, I think I would have done more than just walk. I would have been jumping, running, and maybe even dancing. But Jesus, knowing that this man was beginning a long journey to wholeness, knew that it was best for him to begin by walking. Yes, he had been healed, but he still needed to be made whole.

Our Christian journey begins when we acknowledge our sinfulness, accept Christ's unconditional love and forgiveness, and ask him to come into our lives and walk with us. Like the man at the poolside, we are healed; we take up our mats and begin to walk. But this is not the end of the journey—it's the beginning.

In order to move from walking to dancing, God gives us some practices that help us grow into mature disciples of Jesus Christ. Like a runner training for a marathon, these practices help us build our spiritual muscles and shape us into the image of Jesus Christ—that we might be not only healed, but made whole.

✝ These practices include prayer, worship, journaling, Bible study, and service. We don't work at the practices, they work at us. We don't pray to accomplish the goal of telling God about our lives and needs. We pray so that God can communicate with us and shape us into God's image. We don't study the Bible only to be informed about the Scriptures, but so that we can be transformed as disciples. We don't serve to feel good about helping the less fortunate, but to live the love that Christ commands.

ᚦ Christian practices require sacrifice, commitment, and faith—the sacrifice of our time and desire for personal gain, the commitment to keep going even when we don't see evidence of God working in us, and the faith that God is doing great work in us and will be faithful to complete it.

Story idea
(Refer to your opening story in a similar way.)

I may never learn to dance, but, as my youth reminded me, I am on my way. It will be a journey that will take a little more sacrifice, commitment, and faith than one trip to the arcade. It will be a journey that requires my attention and my energy. But my guess is that it will be worth it.

Wrap it Up

And so, the question comes to each of us today: "Do you want to be made well?" Do you want not only to be healed but to be made whole? Do you want to move beyond the Christian life to the Christlike life? Then start practicing. Make sacrifices that will allow you enough time for Christian practices. Commit to these practices even when they become difficult. And have faith that God will use these practices to shape you into Christlikeness.

ᚦ Do you want to learn to dance? Do you want to be made well? Then rise, take up your mat, and dance!

So What? ᚦ

- How can you train for your walk with God like you train for a sports or music competition?
- What *do* you do to practice your faith? What will you *start* doing to practice your faith?
- How have you experienced God's grace?

Scott McCrary
is the youth minister
at East Cross United
Methodist Church in
Bartlesville, Oklahoma. He is
a graduate of Oklahoma
Baptist University and has been
in full-time youth ministry for
more than ten years. Scott is
married, with one daughter and
one son.

Scott is one of those boisterous,
hilarious-without-trying-too-hard,
loveable youth pastors who has a
huge heart for communicating
gospel truths to students. His
talks are in "teaching point"
or outline form so you'll
have to fill in the blanks
with your own style
and stories.

10. Watch Your Mouth!

The Point: to help youth discover the power of words

The Scripture: "Let no evil talk come out of your mouths, but only what is useful for building up" (Ephesians 4:29a).

Start Talking

Have youth volunteers give a dramatic reading of James 3:1-12. This passage uses illustrations that youth can understand to vividly explain how powerful the tongue and language are. ✒ Then read aloud Ephesians 4:29a and challenge your youth to use language positively.

Story idea
Tell a story of when what you meant to say just didn't come out the right way. I'm sure you have one!

Speak the Word

The Power of Language: Some Teaching Points ✒

☞ We are taught in English class that the same word can have multiple meanings (homonyms).

☞ What is funny to some can be hurtful to others.

☞ Different people can take something you say in entirely different ways.

The Negative Uses of Language: Some Teaching Points ✒

☞ The tongue is a small part of the body; but a single word can be more powerful than any punch of a fist.

☞ Our words can spread quickly like a forest fire—especially gossip. (See James 3:5b.)

☞ Our words not only hurt others, but can negatively affect our present and future lives. (See James 3:6.)

☞ Animals can be tamed, but language can be almost impossible to control. (See James 3:7-8.)

The Positive Uses of Language: Some Teaching Points ✍

☞ Our words are meant to praise God. (See James 3:9.)

☞ We use words to worship, to sing praises, and to talk with God.

☞ We use words to encourage others. (See Ephesians 4:29.)

☞ We use words to express love toward others.

Wrap it Up

Say something like: "You know the saying: ✍ 'You kiss your mother with that mouth?!' Following Christ means deciding to use our words to build up and not tear down. It means using words that bring people together, not words that separate them. The next time you feel the urge to say something mean or negative, think about the power of your words. The damage they will inflict will be lasting. The next time you are about to gossip, pray that God would stop you and speak kindness from your mouth. Words are a gift from God. Use them to build God's kingdom."

Read aloud Ephesians 4:29 again to close.

So What? ✍

🗨 When have you knowingly used words to hurt someone?

🗨 When have you been hurt by what was said about you?

🗨 How can you use your words to build up God's kingdom on earth?

11. Attitude Change

The Point: to help youth find the Christlike attitude within

The Scripture: "Let the same mind be in you that was in Christ Jesus" (Philippians 2:5).

Start Talking

Talk about a new policy that you are enacting called "Attitude Check." Say something like: "From now on when I notice that people are starting to get on one another's nerves, I will yell ✋ 'ATTITUDE CHECK!' When I call for an attitude check, stop what you are doing and yell '1, 2, 3, PRAISE THE LORD!' " ✋ Practice this a few times, and remember to use it again when your youth's attitudes go sour.

Then roleplay some common negative attitudes your youth have given you in the past. For example, "This is boring!" or "That game is stupid" or "I hate when he sings that song!"

Speak the Word

Say something like: ✋ "Our attitude directly reflects our relationship with God. As Christians, God's grace should permeate our lives. Our attitude should be one of gratitude and service for God, who has demonstrated love through Christ."

Movie Idea

A great example of an attitude change is in the movie *Sister Act 2: Back in the Habit*. This movie is full of teenagers with attitudes. Here are three specific scenes to use:

• The first is when Sister Mary Clarence (Whoopi Goldberg) enters the classroom for the first time [23:30-24:35]. This scene provides several examples, but focus the exchange with the student, Rita.

• The second is when Sister Mary Clarence talks to her class about adopting a new attitude [36:10-39:00]. Focus on how Rita once again shows attitude.

• The third is when the class goes to watch the nuns perform at a nursing home [41:25-45:25].

⚓ Signs That an Attitude Needs to be Changed: Teaching Points

☞ Selfishness: Let's talk about what it means to be selfish.

☞ Arrogance: What are some signs of arrogance?

☞ Bitterness: How does bitterness destroy our attitudes?

⚓ The Characteristics of a Christlike Attitude: Teaching Points

☞ Servanthood: Just as Christ served others we are called to serve.

☞ Though humility is often seen as a sign of weakness, Christ demonstrates that humility requires strength.

☞ Obedience to God means humbling ourselves to serve others.

Illustration

A Christian sports camp in Texas created a superhero for its summer camp called "I-Am-3rd Man." This character went around teaching that our attitudes should be such that Jesus comes first, others second, and ourselves last. "I-Am-3rd Man" is an excellent illustration of the attitude we are to have as Christians.

Wrap It Up
Read aloud Philippians 2:5.

Say something like: "When we profess Christ as our Lord, we make a commitment to imitate his life. This means laying aside our bad attitudes and taking on the attitude of Christ, which means loving others. ⚓ Even when we feel like having a bad attitude, we are called to praise the Lord." Yell "Attitude Check!" and let the youth respond "1, 2, 3, Praise the Lord!"

So What? ⚓

☻ Tell about a time when you remember having a terrible attitude.

☻ What does it mean to "let the same mind be in us that is in Christ Jesus"?

12. Friend or Foe?

The Point: to help youth discover true friendship

The Scripture: "Shadrach, Meshach, and Abednego answered the king, 'O Nebuchadnezzar, we have no need to present a defense to you in this matter. If our God whom we serve is able to deliver us from the fiery furnace of blazing fire and out of your hand, O king, let him deliver us. But if not, be it known to you, O king, that we will not serve your gods and we will not worship the golden statue that you have set up' " (Daniel 3:16-18).

Start Talking

Say something like: "One of the biggest struggles of growing up is discerning true friendship. So many times 'best friends' become distant because of small disagreements or changing interests. You can probably think of examples in your own life of persons whom you once thought to be great friends who are now no more than acquaintances. ✆ Friends are gifts from God. When we see one another as allies on our journeys of faith, we will be more careful not to let our friendships fade."

Speak the Word

#1 Truth about Friendship: ✆ True friends don't turn their backs on each other in a time of trial. (See Job 6:14-30.)

Say something like: "What do we know about Job? The story of Job is a great example of how friends can turn their backs on a friend in a time of trial. Everything that can go wrong in life goes wrong for Job. Everything that Job has in life is taken from him. Job's friends assume that he is being punished for sinning against God and challenge him to admit his sin. As Job continues to defend his innocence, his friends gradually pull away and abandon him."

#2 Truth about Friendship: ✆ True friends stick together when times are difficult. (See Daniel 3.)

GSN—The Network for Games has a show titled *Friend or Foe*. Contestants on this show compete in teams of two. When a team is eliminated from the game, they come to a trust box to determine whether or not they will split the money they have won. Each player secretly votes "friend" or "foe," but is first given a minute to explain why his or her partner should choose "friend." If both players vote "friend," they split the money; if both vote "foe," neither gets the money. But if one votes "friend" and the other votes "foe," the player who votes "foe" wins *all* the money. Often, contestants will tell their teammates to trust them, then succumb to the temptation of winning all of the money and vote "foe."

Say something like: "The story of Shadrach, Meshach, and Abednego is an example of friends committed to sticking together. Standing before King Nebuchadnezzar (NEB-uh-kuhd-NEZ-uhr), these three friends are faced with some difficult choices. Will they forsake their God? Will they forsake one another? Will they stick together in faith, even if it means being sentenced to death?"

#3 Truth About Friendship: True friends forgive friends who fail them. (See John 21:15-25.)

Say something like: "Jesus' forgiveness of Peter is the perfect example of someone forgiving a friend who has failed him. Jesus, before his arrest, predicts Peter's denial. Peter, of course, denies knowing Jesus three different times. Three times! But Jesus asks Peter three times, 'Simon son of John, do you love me?' Just as Christ forgives, true friends should forgive."

#4 Truth About Friendship: True friends love each other at all costs.

Say something like: "The Bible includes many stories of what it means to be a true friend. Jesus said it best when he said that the greatest two commandments are to love God and to love your neighbor as yourself (Matthew 22:36-40). Jesus wasn't talking about just loving the people in the house next door. He meant that Christian friendship involves loving everyone, no matter how painful or how difficult. We are called to this kind of love."

Wrap It Up

Have your youth pair off. (You may need to pair off with one of the youth so that numbers will be even.) Instruct the partners to join hands and take turns praying aloud that God will make your youth group a place where true friendship abounds. After a minute or so, tell youth to find different partners and to pray again. Continue until each youth has prayed with every other youth. Express to your group how important it is for each of them to be an example of true friendship in their schools and everyday lives. Assure them that you will pray for them, because true friendship can be difficult.

So What?

- What makes a person a "best" friend?
- What does your faith in Christ have to do with your friendships?
- What kind of friend does Christ call you to be?

Story

I once heard a story about Minnesota Vikings quarterback, Daunte Culpepper. When Daunte was at Marshall University, he injured his ankle in the middle of a key conference game. Since the game was so important, he continued to play. Between each play two or three of Daunte's offensive linemen would carry him down the field to the next play so that he wouldn't have to put any extra pressure on his ankle. I don't know whether this story is true, but it makes an important point: True friends carry us when we need help.

13. Dating

The Point: to help youth apply their faith to decisions about dating

The Scripture: "Do not let loyalty and faithfulness forsake you; bind them around your neck, write them on the tablet of your heart. So you will find favor and good repute in the sight of God and of people. Trust in the LORD with all your heart and do not rely on your own insight. In all your ways acknowledge him, and he will make straight your paths" (Proverbs 3:3-6).

Start Talking

Tell a funny story about your own dating experiences. If you're married, tell a funny story about dating your spouse.

Say something like: "Reality TV has pushed dating and love to a new level. (Or, should we say, a new 'low'?) In biblical times, marriages were arranged based on lineage and economics. Dating as we know it didn't even exist. But the Bible can still help us make wise decisions when it comes to dating."

Speak the Word

Talk for a minute about the old-fashioned concept of courtship. If a boy wanted to court a girl, he would go to her home and spend time with her family. Make up a funny story about one of your boys spending an evening with one of your girl's families.

Ask your group: "Why do we date?" They may give answers such as "to fit in" or "because my friends date." Sadly many youth date only in hopes of fulfilling a need to feel wanted. Self-esteem plays a huge role in dating. And most teenagers feel that in order to be normal they must date.

Now ask: "What are the long-term purposes of dating?" They may give answers such as "to ultimately find the person that I want to marry" or "to discover characteristics I want in a spouse."

Reality TV's Advice On Dating ⌐

Example 1: *The Bachelor* and *The Bachelorette* (Individuals seek their true love from a pool of twenty-five contestants.)

Teaching Point: Viewers usually see each season's bachelor or bachelorette make out with just about every one of his or her potential mates. Use this show as a springboard to talk about kissing. Ask youth what they think about the multiple make-out sessions that take place in every episode. Ask: "Is kissing that big of a deal?" Many youth will answer "no." Ask them to think about if, or when, they have kissed someone they were dating. Have them compare that dating experience to dating someone they didn't kiss (if they have had such a relationship). Ask: "Which relationship was or would be harder to get over?" Most will say the one in which they kissed someone.

Talk about how our faith can help us make good decisions when it comes to kissing or more on dates. Some people say, "I wouldn't do anything on a date that I wouldn't do in front of my parents—or Jesus." While that rule is not helpful for everyone, it does point to the fact that youth can set boundaries before a difficult situation arises, so that they will automatically know how to act.

⌐ Read aloud Proverbs 3:3-6.

Say something like: "Whenever you're thinking about dating someone, I challenge you to read this passage over and over again. Trust in God to help you make good decisions. Wear your faith like a necklace—like something that is always with you for guidance and courage."

Pick My Date Game

Select one contestant for a game, and ask this person to leave the room. Then select three "suitors" ("suitor #1," "suitor #2," and "suitor #3") of the gender opposite the contestant's. Bring the contestant back into the room, but make sure he or she is blocked off and cannot see the suitors. Then have the contestant ask the suitors a series of ridiculous questions you have prepared beforehand (similar to those used on *The Dating Game*). After the contestant has asked all of the questions, have him or her whisper in your ear which person he or she would most like to go on a date with. Then announce to everyone that the Pick My Date Game has a twist, and that the audience will decide whom the contestant will date. Have the audience vote with a show of hands, then introduce the contestant to the two suitors who were not selected. Finally, show the contestant and the winning suitor to a special place where they can sit and enjoy a soda while you teach this lesson on dating.

Example 2: *Meet My Folks* and *Who Wants to Marry My Dad*

Teaching Point: What a radical idea: Parents select who their kids will date (sounds kinda Old Testament). From my perspective, in only one episode of *Meet My Folks* did the parents choose the date their kid actually wanted. The parents always blew it and sent their child on a bad date! But the tables were turned on *Who Wants to Marry My Dad*. The contestant's adult children picked the woman they felt was best for their father, though she was not the woman he was most attracted to. Maybe those on the outside looking in *do* have a little better insight! ❧ How can our friends and family help us make wise decisions about dating?

Example 3: *For Love or Money* and *Joe Millionaire*

Teaching Point: These shows are based on deceit. In both shows the main contestant could not reveal how much money was at stake. Talk about why honesty and trust are keys to a great relationship. ❧ Is money more important than relationships?

Example 4: *Mr. Personality* and *Average Joe*

Teaching Point: These shows have the contestant choose between "average" and "hot" dates. Cut out two pictures (one of a model, the other one of an average-looking person). Ask youth which person is more likely to be someone's first choice for a date. ❧ How often do we look beyond a person's appearance? Challenge youth to examine what they really look for in a date.

Wrap It Up

Say something like: "Dating on reality television is hardly representative of *reality*. Most of the winning couples have since broken up. So instead of looking to so-called 'reality TV,' let's look elsewhere when we make decisions about dating. ❧ I challenge you to turn first to the Lord for strength, courage, confidence, and self-control. Trust in the Lord with your whole heart. God will always be there for you."

So What? ❧

- What difficult decisions have you had to make when it comes to dating?
- How can you trust God, instead of your own desires and inclinations, when it comes to dating?
- How can God help you in your dating relationships?

14. The Many Faces of the Media

The Point: to help youth discover the hold the media has on them and not be duped into believing everything they see or hear

The Scripture: " 'All things are lawful,' but not all things are beneficial. 'All things are lawful,' but not all things build up. Do not seek your own advantage, but that of the other" (1 Corinthians 10:23-24).

Start Talking

Ask: "Do you think that downloading music and burning it onto CD's is wrong? Why or why not? Everybody does it, right? Some companies on the Internet even help you do it."

Youth may respond with answers such as: "If it is wrong why do they make CD burners and recordable CD's?" or "It's not wrong if I own the CD or plan to buy it" or "Those artists have plenty of money. Does it really matter?"

Say something like: "The truth is that it does matter. The whole debate about downloading music is a sign that young people are obsessed with music; the music and computer industries know this and exploit it. But music is only one aspect of the media that has a hold on people your age. As Christians we have to take a step back and ask ourselves: How tight a hold will I allow the media to have on me? ᚛ Will I let God determine my values, beliefs, and character, or will I let the entertainment world tell me who I am or should be?"

Speak the Word

᚛ Read aloud 1 Corinthians 10:23-24. Say something like: "Some issues that we wrestle with today seem to fall into a scriptural gray area. Right and wrong is not always clear-cut. This Scripture says that while we have the freedom to choose to do what we want, not all of our decisions—even those that are legal—are beneficial, constructive, or fair to others or ourselves."

#1 The Impact of Music: Play a game of "Name That Song". Ask your group to name the artist who recorded a popular song when you say the song's title. Then ask your youth some Bible trivia questions. Compare their knowledge of popular music with their knowledge of the Bible.

Beforehand, gather some CD inserts or booklets with lyrics of popular songs. Choose some lyrics that are not explicitly Christian but that have a good message. Read the lyrics or play the song, and talk with your youth about what they like or don't like about the song's lyrics. Do the same thing with a song whose lyrics have a negative message.

Talk about how what we listen to affects us. Refer again to the Scripture. Yes, we can listen to any kind of music we want to, but is the music we listen to beneficial to our relationships with God?

Say something like: "Music is a gift from God. Throughout the Bible music is used to praise God. It's also an example of creative self-expression and a medium for prophetic voice. But problems arise when we stop thinking for ourselves about what 'good music' is and let MTV or a popular website or radio station define what music we like. Sometimes we enjoy a song's tune or beat even when the lyrics are less than desirable. But when we listen to music with destructive messages, we can't just assume that the words will have no affect on us. I challenge you to think about how your music choices affect your walk with God. Your decisions about music are between the two of you."

#2 Movies and Television: Say something like: "Ask yourself, Do the movies and television shows that I watch truly affect me? Do you think that what we see on movies or TV shows can be helpful or harmful? How?

"Think about it. Some of the movies most popular among young people are filled with casual sex, graphic violence, exploitation of women, and foul language—and I mean foul! Why do movies made for a teenage audience need sex, violence, and dirty language to be a hit at the box office?

"What about television shows? What positive or negative messages do you get from your favorite shows? How does watching these shows bring you closer to Christ?"

Wrap it Up

Say something like: "Whether we admit it or not, the media has a strong hold on much of our lives. Why do we care about name brands? Because advertisements tell us to. How do we know what is cool? Because magazines tell us. Why do our brains think it's better to be thin and beautiful or tall and buff than plain and homely? Because that's what the world tells us.

"Somewhere along the way messages have filled our minds that often speak louder than Christ's message for us: ✺ that we are beautiful, beloved, accepted, worthy, wanted just as we are— children of a beautiful God.

"So how can we live in a media-driven culture and still claim our Christian identity and adhere to godly values? To start with, we can recognize the current hold that media has on us. What we ignore or don't know about we can't stop! Make a point to really think about the content of the music you listen to, the movies you watch, and the TV shows you're addicted to. How do these things build up or tear down your faith?

✺ "I want to challenge you to think. God doesn't tell us to sell our TV's and stereos or to give up movies all together. God says that everything is lawful. However, we have to discern what is beneficial for building up our faith. Christ calls us to be in the world, but not to become 'of' the world. That means not letting the world tell us who or whose we are. We know that in Christ we belong to God. The world cannot have a greater hold on us than God. I'm challenging you to think and make good choices when it comes to the entertainment industry. Don't let the world tell you what's good for you. Stand apart and make good choices."

So What? ✺

- What kinds of messages do your favorite TV shows and songs send?
- How are you influenced by what you see on television or in the movies?
- What does it mean to be a Christian in a media-driven society? How does your faith affect how you respond to the media?
- How can our faith influence others for Christ?

15. Is It Real?

The Point: to help youth identify with Nicodemus'
struggle to claim the truth of Christ's message and to help
youth claim Christ's truth for themselves

The Scripture: "Rabbi, we know that you are a teacher
who has come from God; for no one can do these signs
that you do apart from the presence of God" (John 3:2).

Illustration

Have a taste test to determine
"the real thing". Use one
regular soft drink and one diet
soft drink (or two different
brands of regular soft drinks).
Do the taste test just like the
ones we endure in the grocery
store. Hide the drinks behind a
box, and give youth a small
sip of each drink in a small
cup. See whether they can
determine the real thing!

Start Talking

Say something like: "Remember the old
ads for Coca-Cola® claiming, 'It's the real
thing' or 'Can't beat the real thing'? Today
we're going to talk about what determines
whether something is 'the real thing.' "

"Are you someone who wants proof? Do
you have to be absolutely sure that
anything you buy into is 'legit'? I'm sure
most of you could recite John 3:16 from
memory if I asked you to right now, but
today we're going to talk about the story
surrounding that verse. John 3:16 is
actually part of Jesus' answer to one man's
search for the real, true God."

Speak the Word

Ask three volunteers **to read aloud John 3:1-21** in parts. Assign
the roles of Jesus, Nicodemus, and Narrator each to a different
volunteer.

Some Teaching Points on Nicodemus

Nicodemus: The Teacher

Nicodemus was an intelligent and respected leader and a teacher.
He had studied the Scriptures and was familiar with the
prophecies about the Messiah. ⸙ This guy knew his stuff.

64

Nicodemus: The Student

Even with all of his knowledge, ✞ Nicodemus was still a seeker. He desired a deeper sense of spirituality. Nicodemus came in secret, at night, seeking Christ. He was searching for the real thing—for a relationship with God that was truly fulfilling.

Nicodemus Tried to Understand With Reason Instead of Faith

Nicodemus understood there was something special about Jesus, but he had trouble making the leap of faith. When Jesus spoke of being "born again," ✞ Nicodemus relied on his reason to understand. He challenged Jesus' assertion that a person could be born again. In the end he was stuck with the question: "How can this be?" Nicodemus wanted to understand, but reason kept him from taking that extra step to faith.

Nicodemus Was Persistent in His Pursuit

Nicodemus continued to ask questions. He continued to listen. He didn't just say, "No, this is too much to take in." ✞ Nicodemus was in pursuit of truth.

Wrap It Up

Say something like: "Maybe you're like Nicodemus: seeking Christ when no one else is looking and asking for more proof and understanding. Maybe you need Christ to convince you that he is 'the real thing.' This is what Christ says to you: [**Read aloud John 3:11-21.**] ✞ Christ writes his truth on our hearts. Sometimes reason keeps us from understanding how Christ writes on our hearts; but we can choose to take a leap of faith and to believe. Close your eyes right now and take a minute to listen for Christ saying to you, ✞ 'I am the real thing.' "

So What? ✞

- ◈ In what ways are you like Nicodemus? What do you have trouble believing or understanding?
- ◈ How are you different from Nicodemus?
- ◈ How does the truth of Christ live in you?

16. Casting Stones

The Point: to help youth discover grace and the freedom to sin no more

The Scripture: "Let anyone among you who is without sin be the first to throw a stone at her. . . . Go on your way, and from now on do not sin again" (John 8:7, 11b).

Story idea

If you feel comfortable, tell your group about a time when you really messed up and felt horrible. Convey to your group the depth of God's grace you experienced in that situation.

Start Talking

Say something like: ⌖ "The story of the adulteress is a classic story of God's grace toward humankind. Imagine feeling as though the entire world were against you. Imagine thinking that your life were about to end because of one mistake that you made. Sometimes the guilt we feel when we mess up can make us feel pretty low."

Speak the Word

Read aloud John 8:1-11. Say something like: "This story teaches us that God's grace is not reserved for a select few. Through Christ, grace is available to all of us, even when we can't comprehend it.

"Have you ever felt as though your sin was too much for God to forgive? The story of Jesus stepping in to save the woman caught in adultery shows that God's grace is possible in all situations."

⌖ **Read aloud Ephesians 3:20-21.** Say something like: "God is in the business of doing the unimaginable."

⌖ **Read aloud Romans 8:35-39.** Say something like: "Nothing can separate us from the love of God.

"The story of the adulterous woman also teaches us that we cannot do what we want when we want, just because we know that we will receive God's grace. Jesus said to the woman, 'Go and sin no more.' She no longer had to be a slave to her sin. She no longer had to feel the guilt and shame. She no longer had to face insurmountable fears.

"Christ forgave the woman and sent her away free from her inclination to sin. Christ does the same for us. We don't have to be a slave to the things that keep us trapped in sin. We don't have to feel the guilt and the shame. ⌖ In Christ, we are forgiven and freed from our sin."

Wrap It Up

Say something like: "What do you think about this woman's story? How do you relate to the woman? How do you relate to the angry judging mob? Let's take a moment to examine our lives." (Allow an adequate amount of silence in between the following questions.) ⌖ Ask:

☞ What are you judged for?
☞ Why or how do you judge others?
☞ What is keeping you from living a life free from sin?

Say something like: "Think about the plot of this story: The woman feels the immense weight of sin, then the fear of being stoned, and finally the elation of being freed from her sinful life. This is the story of each of our lives. This is how God's grace works in our lives. We sin and feel guilt. We fear the consequences of our actions, but when we remember that ⌖ Christ does the imaginable—he forgives us and frees us."

So What? ⌖

💋 Where do you see yourself in this story?
💋 What strikes you the most about this story?
💋 How will you live differently when you experience freedom from sin?

Reginald Blount

is Instructor of Christian Education and Youth Ministry at Garrett-Evangelical Theological Seminary and Director of Faith Passage, a yearlong spiritual and leadership development program for high school youth. Rev. Blount also serves as pastor of Trinity African Methodist Episcopal Church in Waukegan, Illinois. He is a candidate in the Garrett-Evangelical/Northwestern University joint program in Religious and Theological Studies. His dissertation explores the role of African American churches in the identity formation of African American youth. Rev. Blount is a strong advocate for youth and their issues and concerns, particularly issues of faith and commitment to the gospel of Christ. He desires to work with all persons and faith communities committed to envisioning new and creative ways to minister to, with, and on behalf of youth.

Imagine a deep, loud, passionate voice as you read through Reggie's sermons. The talks in this section are transcripts of sermons that Reggie has given to various groups of youth over the years. As you read you'll hear the passion in his voice. Use these talks as ideas and springboards to develop your own passionate message for your particular group. These sermons will no doubt, inspire you in your ministry and call to minister with youth.

17. Defeating Dream-Busters

The Point: to help youth rely on God when they feel like the world is against them

The Scripture: "They said to one another, 'Here comes this dreamer. Come now, let us kill him and throw him into one of the pits; then we shall say that a wild animal has devoured him, and we shall see what will become of his dreams' " (Genesis 37:19-20).

Start Talking

Beloved, I have no doubt that there is a word from the Lord for all God's children assembled here today. You know what it means to be disappointed. You know how it feels to trust someone only to be betrayed or let down. You know how it feels to be talked about. You know how it feels to be teased and bullied. You know what it's like to be dissed and rejected. You know the pain of being lied to. You've been hurt and confused by self-righteous folks who tell you to live one way while they live another way.

Beloved, many of you know sadness. Many of you know grief. Many of you know depression. Many of you know frustration. Many of you know anger. Many of you know pain and are in need of God to speak to your situation and love all your hurt away.

You want to call on God to heal and restore and renew and revive you and to make you whole. You are looking for God to provide a breakthrough. You are looking for God to overcome anything and everything that hinders you from moving forward, making progress, or achieving your purpose. So, young people, I want to say a word to you today about defeating and breaking through the barrier of dream-busters.

Speak the Word

Beloved, Genesis 37:5 tells us that Joseph had a dream. Now this was not just any kind of dream. This was not just some crazy vision that messed with him while he was asleep; this was not a dream Joseph could not remember the next morning. No, beloved, God allowed Joseph to dream of his future—to better understand his purpose in life. In this dream, God gave Joseph a glimpse of the work God had already prepared for him.

What are your dreams? Do you dream about what you want to do or whom you want to be like? Beloved, I want you to know that God has already prepared your dream. You are God's masterpiece. You are God's work of art. And you were designed just the way you are for a reason.

If you don't remember anything else, remember that you are God's masterpiece! You are God's great work of art. But the magnificence of God's artwork cannot be seen in your outer appearance (though all of you are beautiful in God's sight). Rather, God created a great masterpiece inside each of you. Inside of you, God created love. Inside of you, God created joy. Inside of you, God created peace. And inside of you, God created goals and dreams. God has placed within each of you a purpose, a reason for which you were born.

None of you are accidents. None of you were born by mistake. Some of you may have taken your parents by surprise, but not God. God wanted you here. God needs you here. Before any of you were born God was thinking about you and your destiny. Beloved, you are God's handiwork, God's masterpiece, created in Christ Jesus to do good works that God has prepared in advanced for you.

Young people, I need you to hear me and believe me, because there are powers that would love for you not to know how special you are. These powers would love for you to doubt that you are a masterpiece. These powers would love for you doubt that God gave you dreams. These powers would love for you to think that you're not special. These powers would love for you to think you have no purpose in life. These powers will send people and situations into your life to be dream-busters, people and situations whose sole purpose is to kill the dreams within you.

The Bible says that Joseph had a dream and that, when he told his brothers about his dream, they hated him even more than they already did. Joseph's brothers were jealous; they were jealous of Joseph's relationship with their father, and they were now jealous of Joseph's dreams.

Beloved, there will be people who are jealous: jealous of your relationship with God and jealous of the dreams that God has given you. And, when people are jealous, they will do whatever they can to mess things up. They will tell you that you don't need to come to church. They will tell you that you don't have to read your Bible. They will tell you that you don't have to pray. They will tell you that you're missing out on all the fun. They'll call you "church girl" or "church boy." They'll laugh; they'll tease; they may even bully.

Beloved, I'm here to tell you that they are just jealous. These dream-busters want something that you have. They can't explain it; all they know is that something is different about you. ⚕ They see God's love shining through. They see God's joy shining through. They see God's peace in and all around you. They see God's masterpiece and, instead of claiming God for themselves, they want to destroy what you have, to bring you down to their level. But the Bible says, "No weapon formed against you shall prosper" (Isaiah 54:17, NKJV). If you keep believing in who you are and who God is, what others say or do doesn't matter; you shall always be God's child.

Because we want the best for you, we adults sometimes get in God's way. In our efforts to protect you; in our efforts to keep you from hurt, harm, or danger; in our efforts to shield you from rejection and failure; we adults sometimes bust up your dreams.

Wrap It Up

But beloved, no matter how jealous others might be, and no matter what fears those who love us may have, don't forget: Never let go of the fact that you are God's masterpiece, all of you are God's greatest works, created for a purpose. ⚕ God has dreams for you, beloved. Keep on dreaming!

So What? ⚕

- ◈ What dreams God has placed in your heart?
- ◈ How can you stand firm against those who tear you down?

18. Let No One Despise Your Youth

The Point: to help youth discover their God-given gifts and to empower them to use those gifts for God

The Scripture: "Let no one despise your youth, but set the believers an example in speech and conduct, in love, in faith, in purity" (1 Timothy 4:12).

Start Talking

Allow me to lay the foundation by summarizing a few Scriptures for you:

Psalm 139:13-16: God created you, and God didn't just throw you together. According to the psalmist, you are fearfully and wonderfully made. God thought about you and your life long before you got here.

Jeremiah 1:4-8: Jeremiah tells us that before God formed you, before God prepared you to be born, God already knew you. God knew who you were. God knew your laugh; God knew your smile; God knew what trouble you'd get into; God set you apart. Before you were born, God said, "This is what I want him or her to be; this is how I want him or her to serve me." God knew you and gave you a purpose in life before you were born.

Ephesians 1:4-5: Before God created the world, God chose you. Before the creation of the world God was making plans for you.

Ephesians 2:10: Beloved, you are God's workmanship, created in Christ Jesus to do good works that God prepared for you in advance.

☝ I spoke to you about these verses, because I need you to know how special you are to God. You see, before the world was ever created, God was thinking about you. God was planning for your life. God was preparing for your future. God was determining your purpose in life. Before any of you were born, before any of your parents or grandparents were born, God was thinking about you and the dreams God would give you, the destiny God would create for you, the goals and the purpose God would place inside of you. Beloved, you are God's workmanship; you are God's masterpiece, created in Christ Jesus to do good works that God prepared for you.

I believe that this assurance of God's love from the beginning of time was behind Paul's admonition to Timothy, "Let no one despise your youth," or in the New International Version, "Don't let anyone look down on you because you are young" (1 Timothy 4:12, NIV).

Speak the Word

I believe that, in his statement to Timothy, Paul is reminding Timothy that he is God's workmanship—God's masterpiece—created to use his gifts to do the good works that God had prepared for him in advance. So don't allow others to trip with you. Don't give folks authority that they don't have. Don't give people power over your destiny. Don't let people control your dreams. Don't let people steer you away from your purpose for living.

I believe Timothy was confronted with some haters—people who didn't appreciate someone so young being in charge. These people did not appreciate Timothy being the leader God called him to be. They did not appreciate him living out the purpose God had crafted for him. They did not appreciate him doing the good works that God had prepared in advance for him. They probably felt that he hadn't paid his dues, that he didn't have enough life experiences, that he didn't know enough or wasn't wise enough, that he wasn't good enough, that he wasn't capable of doing the work God had prepared in advance for him to do.

But Paul told Timothy that what other folks thought didn't matter; the opinions of others didn't matter. Paul told Timothy not to let anyone tell him what he could do or who he could be. Paul told Timothy, "Don't let haters rule. Set the tone; set an example through what you say, how you live, how you love, how you believe, and the morals that govern your life. Live your life like the masterpiece God created you to be. Don't let haters despise you, look down on you, or sell you short."

But I'm not as concerned about others despising youth as I am about the person you greet in the mirror every morning. You see, that person in the mirror is the biggest hater in many of your lives. Some of you put yourselves down more than others do.

Some of you sell yourselves short more than others do. Some of you despise yourselves more than others do. Some of you convince yourselves that you are inadequate, that you are not prepared, that you are not worthy to be the masterpiece God created you to be. Each and every one of you was created to be a leader, but some of you run from your calling.

Wrap It Up

⚘ Stop being your chief hater. Stop despising who God thought about, crafted, prepared, and called. Life is hard, and it's certainly not fair, but God never promised us an easy life. God never promised us happiness every day. God never promised us a life without issues. But through Jesus Christ, God did promise never to leave you or forsake you. God did promise that we can be more than conquerors. God did promise that in all things, God is working for the good of those who love God and have been called according to God's purpose. God has promised that nothing can separate us from the love of God: "Neither death nor life, neither angels nor demons, neither the present nor the future, nor any powers, neither height nor depth, nor anything else in all creation, will be able to separate us from the love of God that is in Christ Jesus our Lord" (Romans 8:38-39). ⚘ Let no one, especially yourself, despise your youth. You are God's workmanship, you are God's masterpiece. Beloved, start living the life God prepared in advance for you.

So What? ⚘

- When has someone looked down on you because you are young?
- How will you listen to God's voice over the loud voices of your haters?
- What will it take for you to look in the mirror and love the beautiful child of God whom you see?

19. For Such a Time as This

The Point: to help youth experience a sense of calling, passion, and purpose as they live out their faith in this world

The Scripture: "For if you keep silence at such a time as this, relief and deliverance will rise for the Jews from another quarter, but you and your father's family will perish. Who knows? Perhaps you have come to royal dignity for just such a time as this" (Esther 4:14).

Start Talking

🖰 Beloved, I don't know about you, but there are times when I wake up and I ask myself, "How did I get here?" Each of these times, I was fully aware of my surroundings, and I was where I was when I went off to sleep. I just have days when I find myself asking, "How did I get here?" How did a little black boy from Harlem, New York, get to Waukegan, Illinois? How did I go from being a chemical engineer to pastor and professor at a seminary?

I know the Bible tells me that I'm not here by chance. I know that I'm not here by mistake. I know that I'm not here by the luck of the draw. I know that I'm here because God wants me here. But beloved, every now and then, I still find myself asking, "How did I get here and why does God have me here?" Does anyone know what I'm talking about?

Speak the Word

Read aloud Esther 4:14.

At this point Esther, too, has to be asking herself how it is that she finds herself in her position—as both a Jewish woman and a Persian queen—at such a time.

Esther's story is set in the Persian Empire during the rule of Xerxes the Great and is as good or better than any drama or thriller you've ever read. It opens with Xerxes—referred to as "Ahasuerus" (uh-HAS-yoo-ER-uhs), the Hebrew translation of the Persian word meaning "mighty man"—holding one of the drinking parties for which history tells us he was famous. He commands his wife, Vashti, to come his party so that he can show her off. Vashti refuses to be exploited and embarrasses her husband. Xerxes responds by banishing Vashti and initiating an empire-wide search for a new queen. Among the many beautiful and desirable woman Xerxes could take as a wife, Esther finds favor in his heart. Esther is an orphan Jewish girl brought up in the home of her cousin Mordecai, one of Xerxes' court officials.

A subplot develops as Haman, a high official in Xerxes' court, feels that Mordecai has disrespected him. Enraged, Haman vows to have Mordecai, along with the entire Jewish population, executed, exterminated, annihilated. Haman advises Xerxes to eliminate "a certain people" who "do not keep the king's laws." Without thinking, Xerxes approves such genocide. Unbeknownst to Haman, though, Mordecai had recently saved King Xerxes' life by warning him of an assassination attempt. Xerxes is grateful for the warning, but had not immediately rewarded Mordecai.

Mordecai sends a messenger to appeal to Queen Esther, asking her to speak with the king to prevent the annihilation of her people. Esther knows that only those who have been invited can get an audience with the king. Entering the king's court without an invitation—even if you're the king's wife—is a crime punishable by death. Mordecai reminds Esther that a way will be made for God's people, and that if she does not act, her people will not survive. She must consider whether God had taken her from orphan Jew to Queen of Persia so that she could deal with this very situation.

Esther decides to break the law and see the king. She courageously declares, "If I perish, I perish" (Esther 4:16b). Esther falls at the king's feet and creatively reveals Haman's plot. Ultimately Haman, not Mordecai, is executed, and the Jewish people are allowed to defend themselves against their enemies. Esther is the catalyst who reverses her people's fortunes. Beloved, could it be that we all are here for such a time as this?

Charles Wesley, brother of John Wesley, the founder of Methodism, wrote hundreds of hymns. One of those great hymns, "A Charge to Keep I Have," reminds us:

> A charge to keep I have, a God to glorify,
> a never dying soul to save and fit it for the sky.

To serve the present age, my calling to fulfill;
O may it all my powers engage to do my master's will.

✝ Beloved, I believe that God is calling us for such a time as this, to serve the present age. The harvest God is sending us to gather is a present-day harvest. God calls us to present day people, present day situations, present-day issues, and present-day concerns that are in need of present day healing and eternal salvation by an everlasting God.

Mordecai's response to Esther is clear: God's work will be done, with us or without us. God's vision will be fulfilled. What God wills will come to pass. ✝ We can be silent if we want to. We can do nothing if we want to. We can keep ignoring our call if we want to. We can bury our talents, not use our gifts, or refuse to share our witness if we want to. Mordecai said we can choose to be silent if we want to, but that relief and deliverance are going to come, even if God has to call someone else. ✝ But beloved, could it be that God has brought us to this place for such a time as this?

Wrap It Up

Beloved, it is God's will to bring relief and deliverance to our communities. There is still homelessness among us. There is still poverty among us. There are still racism and classism and sexism and many other "isms" among us. There are still youth shattering their lives with drug and alcohol use. Our society is becoming more and more aware of the debilitating affects of teenage depression. God's vision is that our faith communities will rise up and take a stand and serve the present age.

Beloved, we have a calling to fulfill. And just because you are young does not mean that God does not have a role for you to play, a cause for you to fight for, or a mission for you to serve. There is still a charge to keep. There is still a God to glorify. Beloved, there is still work to do for such a time as this.

So What? ✝

- What is your role in the present day work of God?
- To what is God calling you?
- What do you think of when you hear that you have a mission "for such a time as this"?

20. It Takes a Village

The Point: to help youth discover their roles in the body of Christ

The Scripture: "For just as the body is one and has many members, and all the members of the body, though many, are one body, so it is with Christ" (1 Corinthians 12:12).

Start Talking

Kwanzaa is a cultural holiday celebrated from December 26 through January 1. The holiday affirms the cultural identity of African Americans and strengthens community through African cultural values. ◌ These values are summarized in Kwanzaa's Seven Principles, or *Nguzo Saba* (each value is named by the appropriate Swahili word), which are: ◌ *umoja* (unity); ◌ *kujichagulia* (self-determination); ◌ *ujima* (collective work and responsibility); ◌ *ujamaa* (cooperative economics); ◌ *nia* (purpose); ◌ *kuumba* (creativity); and ◌ *imani* (faith). Although Kwanzaa is a cultural rather than religious holiday, its values complement Christian values. Today's Scripture is an excellent example of the third of Kwanzaa's Seven Principles, *ujima*.

Ujima means that through unity we must build and maintain our community. *Ujima* means doing things for and taking care of others. *Ujima* understands the importance of community and that every member of a community has a part to play. ◌ *Ujima* understands that every person is needed for a village to thrive.

Speak the Word

Instead of using the village as a metaphor or illustration, Paul uses the human body, which I believe also expresses the spirit of *ujima*. Paul explains that the body has many parts and that all the parts are needed if the body is going to work well. Every member, every part of the body is vital and necessary. If the body is going to function properly, then all the members need to be healthy, working well, and working together. If one of your arms could not function, or if one of your legs had been amputated, or if you were unable to see or hear, people would say you had a disability. ⚕ Beloved, when the village does not use all of its members fully—when the body of Christ does not use all of its members fully—then the church is disabled and unable to live out *ujima*, or collective work and responsibility. We are unable to serve God and God's people to our fullest potential. We are unable to truly build our church in the way that God calls us to.

That's why, beloved, I am concerned that we, as a church, neglect your gifts as young people. Now please don't get me wrong. I believe that we do a great job of loving you and supporting you and offering you encouragement when you imitate us well. We do a great job of teaching you to be carbon copies of us. But I wonder, how well are we making room for the gifts you already have within you now? I believe that many of God's churches, sometimes knowingly, but many times unknowingly, tell youth that they must first pay their dues to become a member of the body of Christ. Think about it. With love and sincerity, we look at youth like yourselves and tell them that they are the church of tomorrow. With love and sincerity, we say that our children are our future. But we rarely stop and consider that ⚕ God has equipped youth to be the church of today.

Young people, how many of you believe in Jesus? How many of you have asked Jesus to come live in your hearts? If you have done so, the Bible says that you are a part of God's family, a part of God's village, and a part of God's body right now, and that God has given each and every one of you a special gift to share with the body, to share with the village, *now*. I want to help you discover that gift and to make room for it in the church now, even if your gifts are different from what some adults think the church needs.

Beloved, when children are baptized, they become right then and there members of the body. Young people are a vital part of the church and have gifts that support the body of Christ.

You may not want to invite your friends to church because church is not always kid-friendly. Many churches lack energy and excitement. I want to tell you that you can make a difference in the life of your church. You should be on ministry teams and committees. You should be involved in decision-making. You have a voice. If you don't feel comfortable inviting your friends to church, you need to talk to your pastor. Beloved, God has made you an indispensable part of the body and you have a voice.

To live out the principle of *ujima*, to truly engage in collective work and responsibility, to truly be the body of Christ—the village God has called us to be—we must make room for all the gifts that God has provided for all the members of this body because, ⌁ "God arranged the members in the body, each one of them, as he chose" (1 Corinthians 12:18).

Wrap It Up

I have a message for you young people: You have responsibilities. Just like you have chores at home to keep your family household running well, you also have responsibilities to God's house so that it can run well. None of you are too young to be responsible for helping the church thrive. God has blessed each and every one of you with a gift that can build up the church. Help the adults in the church figure out how to be more youth-friendly. Help the adults figure out how to increase the energy and excitement so that other people your age will want to come to church. Use your gifts to help those who are in need. The church needs you.

If we are truly God's body, we can't say that we don't need one another. Youth can't say that they don't need adults; and adults can't say that they don't need youth. Bring to worship your energy and your excitement about God and what you know God is doing in your lives. Help us praise and glorify God. You see, you are not the church of tomorrow. You are full members of God's church right now!

So What? ⌁

- How does the word "village" describe the church?
- How does the idea of the "body of Christ" describe the church?
- What part of Christ's body are you?
- How will you use your role in body of Christ to build up the church?

21. Power in a Name

The Point: to help youth understand that each of them is named a beloved child of God

The Scripture: "Then Jesus asked him, 'What is your name?' He replied, 'My name is Legion; for we are many' " (Mark 5:9).

Start Talking

There is power in a name. Beloved, I believe that power is something we tend to take too lightly, something we are not always mindful of. I don't think we are always aware that there is something powerful, something commanding, something compelling, something defining about a name.

For you see, beloved, a name defines. A name determines. A name labels. A name designates. A name characterizes. A name describes. A name depicts. A name identifies. O beloved, there is wonder-working power in a name; our names tell the world who we are.

Speak the Word

You see, a name give us our identity, which immediately presents us with a potential problem; for you see, beloved, we never really get to name ourselves. Others name us, others label us, others try to define us, others attempt to describe us.

We are first named by our parents—named after a parent or a relative or favorite movie star or historical or biblical figure; or we are named based on how our parents were feeling when we were born. We are also named by our communities. How many of us have nicknames we can't get rid of? And, yes beloved, we are also named by the dominant, larger society. Too often these names are not names that build us up, or that offer support, but names that work to tear us down.

Oh beloved, all of these names collectively shape our identity and our understanding of who we are.

Did you know that one of the pivotal questions we must answer in life is, "Who Am I?" Given the many names competing to shape our sense of being, is it any wonder that this question is often very difficult to answer? Am I the person I am at school? Am I who I was at the last party I attended? Am I the person I am when I go to church? Am I the person I am when I am at home? Am I who my parents say I am? Am I who society says I am?

Read aloud Mark 5:1-13.

Jesus has just made his way through a storm on the Sea of Galilee; and as Jesus climbs out of the boat in the country of the Gerasenes (GER-uh-seens), the demoniac—the town's outcast, the town's embarrassment—runs out to meet him. The demoniac has been labeled, named, identified by his neighbors as a bona fide mental case. Society has tried repeatedly to bind him, but the man keeps breaking his chains. Unable to find refuge, unable to find peace, unable to find comfort amid his torment at the hands of "civilized" society, the demoniac is driven to live alone in the tombs, alone in the cemetery. As he approaches Jesus—crying for help on the inside, but denying the need for help on the outside, as most tormented souls do—he tells Jesus to leave him be.

But Jesus, looking beyond the man's faults to meet his needs, asks the tormented man, "What is your name?" And the demoniac answers, "Legion; my name is Legion," for this man is possessed by thousands of demons. The demons are his names, his identities, who he is made to believe that he is—many personalities, many identities, living a life of chaos and confusion, trapped, frustrated, repressed, confined, vulnerable, restrained and bound by outsiders, vulnerable, with no sense of purpose, no sense of direction, no sense of call, no insight, no clue about his reason for being. His only identity is "demonic."

When Jesus asks the Gerasene demoniac his name, the man names his problem, his predicament, his torment—his name is Legion. He can name his problem but, sadly, cannot give his real name. He cannot share his true identity, because it is lost among so many other identities, all of which are inhuman, corrupt, depraved, destructive, painful, torturous.

Sadly, I believe that many young people today are seen as America's Gerasene demoniacs. Many youth suffer from chaos and confusion in their souls. Many young people have no sense of purpose, no notion of call or vocation, no clue about their reason for being. All they have are the wrong names shaping their sense of identity. Names like shiftless, lazy, good-for-nothing, irresponsible, inferior, mindless, won't amount to anything, liar, thief, thug, gangsta, trouble-maker, dangerous, and violent. It doesn't surprise me that a number of young folk have made lives for themselves that live up to these horrible names. You see we often live up to the expectations of those who teach and shape us.

But even amid the chaos, turmoil, and confusion there is still good news. I believe Jesus is asking our young people today, "What is your name?" Jesus is asking you to take stock of who is naming you and whose expectations you allow to shape your identity. Jesus is calling you to a new identity. Jesus is calling you to claim the identity you had before the demonic names possessed you. ⦿ Young people, Jesus is telling you that if anybody asks you who you are, tell them that you are a child of God.

Our true identities are lost when we define ourselves by *whom* others say we are, rather than by *whose* we really are. The Gerasene demoniac was transformed by having a little talk with Jesus. ⦿ We need to know that God is still in the business of giving us new names and new identities. God changed Jacob's name from Jacob (which means "schemer") to Israel, providing Jacob and his descendants a legacy, a personhood, and a heritage. God changed an outspoken, impetuous fisherman named Simon, and renamed him Peter, "the rock" on which Christ built his church. God took a Christian-hating Pharisee named Saul, and renamed him Paul, charging him to bring good news to the Gentiles. God is in the new-naming business and calls you to come and claim a new name. Claim the identity God that has prepared for you.

Wrap It Up

⦿ Beloved, the demons that tell us that we are nothing are fierce. But we serve a Savior who knows how to come through the storms, calm them, and drive the demons away. Claim the name that God has for you! There is power in that name!

So What? ⦿

- What is the story behind your name?
- Have you ever felt as though society was trying to give you a new name? How and why did others try to give you this name?

Lillian Smith
is the director
of campus ministries
and Ministries with
Women and Persons of Color
for the General Board of
Higher Education and Ministry
of The United Methodist
Church. Prior to her current
position, Lillian served as
campus minister at
Howard University.

Lillian has a incredible way of
relating details and important
truths of Bible passages to
youth in a way that is fun
and engaging. Her talks are
great jumping-off points
from which to delve
into the Scriptures
with youth.

22. David

The Point: to help youth discover David as a biblical hero

The Scripture: "The LORD does not see as mortals see; they look on the outward appearance, but the LORD looks on the heart" (1Samuel 16:7b).

Start Talking

The Top 10 Reasons David is a Hero

10. He was a great poet and musician.

9. He knew he was a sinner but continued to serve God.

8. He brought the Ark of the Covenant to Jerusalem.

7. He was perfect—Not!—but repented.

6. He saved Saul's life even though Saul wanted to kill him.

5. He was courageous enough to kill the giant, Goliath.

4. He united Israel and Judah into one kingdom.

3. He became the most powerful king of Israel.

2. He loved God and wasn't ashamed to show it.

1. He was upright before God, and his heart was right.

Speak the Word

So what about David? Known as a man "after God's own heart" (see 1 Samuel 13:14), David's name means "beloved." Selected as the future king of Israel as a youth, David grew up to be one of the best known and admired biblical heroes. David was God's choice of future king because his heart was right. People questioned God's choice. ☙ But, as we know, the world looks at the outside, while God sees and knows the inside.

Brave beyond measure, David stood up to the giant, Goliath. Goliath had taunted King Saul and the men of Israel. One day, after caring for the sheep and taking supplies to his brothers on the front line, David heard Goliath talking out of the side of his mouth. Maybe you've heard the old saying, ☙ "Don't let your mouth write a check for you that your behind can't cash." Goliath was talking about "defying the army of Israel"—the army of God! (See 1 Samuel 17:10.) David couldn't take it anymore. He was going to do something. So this little guy decided to take on the giant without any armor. He used only his slingshot and some stones. Think about how ridiculous that sounds—a little guy defeating a giant with a slingshot. But we know that with God all things are possible. ❀ And David knew how to use that slingshot. God used David's skill to win a seemingly impossible fight.

Being a king back then was no piece of cake. Unlike modern monarchs, a king back then had to fight. When David became king he had to protect the borders from enemies or attain additional territory to ensure the protection of his people. He had to set an example for his people and execute God's justice in the kingdom. David was up to the task.

Here's a great story about David: When the Ark of the Covenant was returned to Jerusalem, he danced like crazy for God. I bet we will never see Queen Elizabeth or Prince Charles dance in the street before their people. David did. David took off his coat and danced "before the LORD" (2 Samuel 6:16), like he had lost his mind. David's dancing was a public witness of his love and appreciation for God's goodness.

David was not perfect and he knew it; that's why he was such a great king and is such a great example for us today. He wanted most of all to be right with God, but he continued to mess up. Lies, deceit, adultery, murder—David's sins were scandalous. But David repented; and God, in grace and mercy, knew that David's heart was full of love for God. If you read through the Book of Psalms, you can witness the highs and lows of David's relationship with God.

Wrap it Up

Why is David worth talking about today? What is so great about his story? ❀ I want you to know that when God calls you, God will equip you. When God chooses you for a task, God will give you the tools you need. When your heart is right with God, you will know God as David did.

So What? ❀

- ❧ What skill or craft can you use for God?
- ❧ How will you seek God's "own heart"?
- ❧ What would cause you to unashamedly dance for God?

23. Esther

The Point: to help youth seek and gain the courage of Esther

The Scripture: "After that I will go to the king, though it is against the law; and if I perish, I perish" (Esther 4:16b).

Start Talking

Have you ever experienced a "divine set-up?" 🖐 Have you ever felt as though God has guided you, through no effort of your own, into a position of power and influence? This happened to a young woman named Esther. Born into obscurity, Esther became the wife and queen of a Persian king.

Speak the Word

Esther was born with the name *Hadassah* (huh-DAS-uh), meaning "myrtle." Her Persian name, Esther, means "star" and "good fortune." Esther was the descendant of people who had been forced to leave Jerusalem, and she found herself in Persia.

Esther's good fortune began after she was selected, from among many women, to be King Ahasuerus' (uh-HAS-yoo-ER-uhs) new wife. The king's former wife, Queen Vashti, was banished after refusing to grant the then drunk king's request to parade in front of his drunken friends at a party. An orphan, Esther was raised by her cousin, Mordecai, who instructed her to not reveal her Jewish identity. This instruction proved helpful. Persian law prohibited the king to marry a Jewish woman and decreed that he must choose a wife from another prominent Persian family.

Mordecai was a person in the know. He was often in the right place at the right time. Once he heard about and thwarted a plot to kill King Ahasuerus. He later overheard a plot to kill all the Jews in the kingdom. The plan, devised by Mordecai's rival, Haman, was approved the king.

Alarmed, Mordecai sent a message to Queen Esther and challenged her to do something to avert this horrible plan. She would have to speak to the king to secure the deliverance of her people. Esther found herself in a quandary. No one went to see the king without being summoned. Any person who visited the king unannounced could be killed, even the king's wife!

🕊 Would Esther risk her life by entering the king's court? Or would she keep her identity secret while her people were slaughtered? Would she try to save her people or just take care of herself? Mordecai reminded Esther that she, a Jew, was not exempt from this decree. "Do not think that in the king's palace you will escape any more than all the other Jews. For if you keep silence at such a time as this, relief and deliverance will rise for the Jews from another quarter, but you and your father's family will perish. Who knows? Perhaps you have come to royal dignity for just such a time as this" (Esther 4:13-14). What would Queen Esther do?

Esther knew that she needed help to be successful. So she called on the Jewish people for help. 🕊 She instructed Mordecai to "Go, gather all the Jews to be found in Susa, and hold a fast on my behalf, and neither eat nor drink for three days, night or day. I and my maids will also fast as you do. After that I will go to the king, though it is against the law; and if I perish, I perish" (Esther 4:16).

Wrap It Up

A position of power and prestige is meant never just for the satisfaction of the person in power. 🕊 God places you in various situations for a reason. You are with those friends, on that committee or ministry team, on that ball team, or in that classroom for a reason. Wherever you find yourself, God wants and needs you to speak for those who can't speak for themselves. 🕊 God wants you to use your position and prestige to work for justice.

Next time you find yourself in a position to make a difference for the good of others, act for God. Who knows, perhaps God has placed you in this position "for such a time as this."

So What?

- When have you felt as though you were in a situation in which you had to take action?
- When have you been in control of someone else's fate? How did you act?
- How can we gain the courage and resolve of Esther to do the sometimes scary work of God?

Story idea

(This is my story. Use it or a better one of your own.)

When I was younger I'd find myself in various settings where I'd become frustrated because people were silent about issues I felt were unjust or needed addressing. "Why doesn't someone speak up and say something?" I'd ask myself. Finally, it hit me: "Knucklehead, why don't *you* say something?" Oops! *I* was the person who was supposed to say something. My location at the table was not just for show—no quota or affirmative action program arranged my presence there. God placed me there, and, as a result, I was responsible for actively speaking up for people who were not present or whose voices weren't being heard, let alone acknowledged.

24. Shiphrah and Puah

The Point: to empower youth to stand up for what is right, even when it is risky

The Scripture: "But the midwives feared God; they did not do as the king of Egypt commanded them, but they let the boys live" (Exodus 1:17).

Start Talking

Anybody want to guess what a midwife is? No, it's not the middle wife of a polygamist with three wives. No, it's not a wife who is only with her husband during the middle of the week. A midwife is a nurse specially trained to work with women having babies. Midwives help women during their pregnancies, then help them deliver the baby safely.

Speak the Word

You probably know the story of Pharaoh issuing a decree to have all of the newborn Hebrew boys killed. And you probably know that Moses was saved by being sent up the Nile in a basket in hopes that he would live free from the tyranny of Pharaoh.

Pharaoh instructed Shiphrah (SHIF-ruh) and Puah (PYOO-uh), two midwives, to kill all of the newborn Hebrew boys they helped deliver. In a cruel system that sought to kill the life and future of an entire people, these two unlikely women disregarded Pharaoh's decree in order to enable life.

These women defied the unjust government and let the newborn Hebrew boys live. Their names speak of their life-giving compassion. *Shiphrah* means "prolific" or "to procreate." *Puah* means "child bearing" or "joy of parents."

According to early Jewish history, Shiphrah and Puah were the supervisors of a network of midwives who served both the Egyptian and Hebrew women in childbirth. In that case, their instructions to let the boys live possibly could have been carried out by an estimated 500 other midwives who worked in their circle.

When Pharaoh discovered that little boys were being delivered safely, he questioned Shiphrah and Puah. Telling what might generously be considered a "partial truth," they told Pharaoh that because the Israelite women had easier births, the babies were born before midwives arrived to deliver them. What could Pharaoh say? What did he know about childbirth? After being outwitted and defied by these two midwives, he resorted to enlisting other Egyptians to participate in his cruelty.

The question this Scripture poses to us is: ✡ What do you do when the government tells you to do something that is against God's way of doing things? Having to choose between God and government is not a far-fetched scenario, even in this country; the inhumane system of slavery was legal and condoned in this country for 300 years. In this instance, Shiphrah and Puah went against the government and did what they knew was right in God's sight. Even if they were Egyptian-born, they no doubt had come to revere the God of the Israelites. They must have heard the stories about the God of Abraham, Isaac, and Sarah. "But the midwives feared God; they did not do as the king of Egypt commanded them, but they let the boys live" (Exodus 1:17).

✡ I must tell you, there will always be consequences for your actions, whether right or wrong. Shiphrah and Puah still had to answer to Pharaoh. They must have been frightened about what Pharaoh might do to them, but they answered him nonetheless.

What would you do? Would you obey the king? Would you obey God? Who is the source of the ultimate law in your life? Every generation of believers faces this dilemma.

Conductors on the Underground Railroad chose to answer God's call for peace, justice, and freedom for all rather than answering a government that sanctioned slavery. During the Holocaust, countless European Christians risked their own lives by hiding Jewish men, women and children. Each of those individuals put his or her life at risk. ✡ When faced with a similar situation, you may have to risk your life or reputation.

✡ Puah and Shiphrah, for their bravery, found God's favor. "So God dealt well with the midwives; and the people multiplied and became very strong. And because the midwives feared God, he gave them families" (Exodus 1: 20-21). The bravery of these two women gave the enslaved Israelites hope and a future.

Story idea

Tell a story of someone in your community who has taken a stand for his or her faith even though it was risky. You may even want to have a talk time here to discuss the ways in which your students feel that living their faith is risky for them.

Wrap it Up

The story of Moses being saved is definitely better known than the story of Shiphrah and Puah. But we can learn a lot from these two women who risked their lives to do what was right, because they feared and respected God.

So What?

- What current situations can you think of that might require believers to directly oppose governmental policies?
- Have you ever had to choose between God's law and human law? How did you respond to this choice?
- How can you find the courage to stand up for God even when it's risky?

25. Becoming Fruity

The Point: to help youth live the fruit of the Spirit

The Scripture: "The fruit of the Spirit is love, joy, peace, patience, kindness, generosity, faithfulness, gentleness, and self-control. There is no law against such things" (Galatians 5:22-23).

Start Talking

Let's talk fruit. Apples, oranges, and kiwis are some examples of fruit that we like to eat today. In biblical times grapes, figs, and pomegranates were the fruits of choice. Regardless of what fruits we eat, as Christians, we are instructed to bear fruit. That's right.

Jesus said "I am the vine, you are the branches. Those who abide in me and I in them bear much fruit, because apart from me you can do nothing" (John 15:5). How can we bear fruit? you ask. What kind of fruit are Christians supposed to bear? 🖑 How can we become "fruity" Christians?

> ### Story Illustration
> Provide a bowl of fruit. Hold up and describe each piece of fruit in the bowl. For instance, an orange is sweet and juicy. It grows on trees that are really fragrant. You might even give each youth a piece of fruit to eat while you talk.

Speak the Word

Just as fruit reflects the tree or vine that sustains it, so Christians are to bear fruit that outwardly reflects our relationship with Christ and the inner working of the Holy Spirit in our lives and hearts. 🖑 "The fruit of the Spirit is love, joy, peace, patience, kindness, generosity, faithfulness, gentleness, and self-control" (Galatians 5:22-23).

If we are honest, bearing any of these "fruits" without the help of the Holy Spirit is impossible. Who wants to love someone who has lied to you or is dating your ex-boyfriend or ex-girlfriend? Who wants to be kind to someone who has harmed you or a loved one? Not me—not without a whole lot of God's power.

When you hear what the fruit of the Spirit is, you might say to yourself, "This is hard. I just don't think I can possibly possess all of those qualities all the time." Go ahead and tell God. Then ask God to help you. Let's look at each of these qualities and how we can apply each to our lives.

☙ **Love** is the very foundation of how we should live our lives. We are called to love God and our neighbors as ourselves—even our enemies. (Yes, even people you can't stand right now!)

☙ **Joy** is the happiness we get from relationships and love. Joy comes from trusting in God's promises. We are joyful because God loves us, has redeemed us, has reconciled us, and has given us authority "over all the power of the enemy" (Luke 10:19).

☙ **Peace** is difficult to describe. You know when you have peace and when you don't have peace, but putting these experiences into words is another story. To have peace is to be assured that God is still God even when you don't have control over a situation. To have peace is to know without a doubt that God has perfect timing, even though God's timing may be different from yours.

☙ **Patience** is rarely an easy fruit to bear. You may have heard the saying, "God may not come when you want, but God is always on time." The saying reminds us why we should patiently trust God even when we don't see how God's promises are fulfilled.

☙ **Kindness** is usually easy when the recipient of your kindness is also kind to you. It is difficult and requires the help of the Holy Spirit when the recipient is less than loveable.

☙ **Generosity** is defined as the ability to share with or give to others. God wants you to be generous. God wants you to be unselfish with what you have. If God is the source of all that you have, will not God provide you with what you need if you share what you have with someone less fortunate?

☙ **Faithfulness** is easy when life is going well, but, when times get rough, keeping the faith becomes more difficult. Thankfully for us, God is always faithful.

☙ **Gentleness**: Generous, kind, serene, patient, and nonviolent are but a few of the words that help define gentleness. Sometimes gentleness is mistaken for weakness, but keeping a gentle perspective takes a great deal of strength. Think about the last time you wanted to go off on your little brother or sister; surely, it required a lot of strength to remain gentle.

☙ **Self-control** may be the single most difficult fruit of the Spirit to bear. Self-control means thinking before you speak or act. It means knowing when to say "when" in all circumstances.

No matter how hard we try, we cannot bear this fruit on our own. But the good news is that we have a helper, the Holy Spirit. When the Holy Spirit lives in us, when we have turned our lives over to God, others will see the fruit of the Spirit in us. Jesus said that if we don't bear any fruit we'll just wither away. If people can look at us or talk to us without seeing Christ, then we're not living in the Spirit.

Wrap It Up

To exhibit the fruit of the Spirit requires an intentional, daily, ongoing relationship with God. Praying or going to church once a month or year won't do it. Ever notice how a husband and wife who have been married for a long time start to resemble each other? They think alike. They will sometimes even complete each other's sentences or thoughts. That's what happens when we spend time with God. We start acting, talking, and living like God.

Bible reading and study, praying and listening to God, and private and community worship help develop and strengthen our relationship with God. The fruit of the Spirit will help you refrain from angrily cussing someone out and will keep your hormones in check when you are tempted. ☙ Let the world know that Christ lives in you by living the fruit of the Spirit. Besides, being fruity is kind of fun!

So What? ☙

- ☙ Which fruit of the Spirit do you have the hardest time with?
- ☙ How can you allow the Holy Spirit to live more fully in you?
- ☙ How do others know that Christ lives in you?

26. Lessons From Timothy

The Point: to empower youth to be faithful to God even when people look down on them because of their age

The Scripture: "Let no one despise your youth, but set the believers an example in speech and conduct, in love, in faith, in purity" (1 Timothy 4:12).

Start Talking

"Who does this young upstart think he is?" "How has he been given such a prominent role in Paul's ministry?" "He hasn't lived long enough to take on that role?" Timothy, the young colleague of Paul, no doubt heard these questions asked. How could Timothy lead when everyone was giving him a hard time about being too young? What's a young person to do?

I've been there. You have probably been there too. God calls young people to be in active ministry. God even calls children to participate in God's work in the world. So when people question your ministry because of your age, or tell you you're too young, tell them to talk to God about it!

Speak the Word

Timothy played a huge role in the spread of Christianity. His work is mentioned throughout Paul's epistles. His ministry is also mentioned in Acts. (See Acts 16–20.) As a young person Timothy accompanied Paul and Silvanus on missions to Corinth and Thessalonica (THES-uh-luh-NIGH-kuh). Paul wrote two letters to Timothy. Regardless of his age, Timothy was very important to the early spread of Christianity.

Though his father was a Gentile, Timothy was the son and grandson of Jewish women. His mother, Eunice, and grandmother, Lois, no doubt taught him the story of God's faithfulness and promise.

Timothy's witness provides a timeless example of direction and insight for young people who are living out God's call on their lives. ✍ In 1 Timothy 4:6-16 Paul instructs young Timothy to conduct himself in such a way that his actions will not distract from his ministry. People will watch young leaders to find reasons to discredit their integrity or actions or the legitimacy of their call. ✍ In other words, "If you are going to talk the talk, you need to walk the walk."

Have you ever wanted to go off on someone or take your frustrations on others? To do what Paul says, to keep people from looking down on you because you're young, you must keep yourself in check. You must use discretion and wise judgment in your interactions and relationships. ✍ People are always watching. Your challenge is to live as a representative of God in a way that gives God honor. In other words, you have to represent!

Wrap It Up

I hate to put pressure on you, but know that the magnifying glass is focused on you. Live your life in a way that glorifies God and respects others. If you fall, get up. You are not perfect. Watch how you act and what you say. Remember, we are called to exemplify God's love in all that we do and with everyone with whom we interact. You, like Timothy, are God's representative in the world.

✍ You are never too young to be a leader. Don't hide behind your age. Timothy didn't, and God used him as an important leader in the early church. What can God accomplish through your willing heart?

So What? ✍

- ✍ What can you learn about ministry from Timothy's example?
- ✍ How do you react when people look down on you, question you, or underestimate you because of your age?
- ✍ What will God accomplish through you?

27. Jesus as a Youth

The Point: to help youth discover that even Jesus had to deal with parents

The Scripture: "Child, why have you treated us like this? Look, your father and I have been searching for you in great anxiety" (Luke 2:48).

Start Talking

What might Jesus' parents have thought or felt when they couldn't find their son? Were they angry at him or afraid for him? Imagine how shocked and anxious Mary and Joseph must have been when they discovered that their first-born son wasn't with the family caravan as it returned home from Jerusalem. Jesus should be glad that he didn't live in my household. If I had pulled that stunt, it would have been all over for me.

Speak the Word

You might be wondering how Jesus' parents would not have noticed that he had been missing from the group for two days. Jewish people making pilgrimages to Jerusalem often traveled with family members and friends for safety reasons. Large groups deterred robbers. Women and children traveled in one segment of the caravan. The men would travel in another. Because of his age—on the border between childhood and adulthood—Jesus could have been in either section of the group with either parent. Each parent probably thought that Jesus was with the other.

After being away from their son for two days, Jesus' parents frantically returned to Jerusalem and spent an entire day searching the city. ☙ "When his parents saw him, they were astonished; and his mother said to him, 'Child, why have you treated us like this? Look, your father and I have been searching for you in great anxiety' " (Luke 2:48).

☙ Even as a youth Jesus had a passion for the things of God. His response to his parents was priceless: "Why were you searching for me? Did you not know that I must be in my Father's house?" (Luke 2:49). If my parents had been in Mary and Joseph's shoes, I'm sure they would have replied, "What did you say? Have you lost your mind making us worry like that? You couldn't have told someone of your plans? I don't care if you are God's son, you know better! Now come on!"

Jesus was a young person just like you. He had to abide by and negotiate the parent-child relationship. Jesus and his parents had to go through his transition from childhood to manhood. Believe me, growing up isn't easy for anyone. Jesus went through some of the same emotions and challenges that you have or will experience. As a youth he lived out his passion for God's law.

Isn't it amazing that the Messiah, the King of Kings, the Prince of Peace, learned about God from others? He sat in the Temple listening to rabbis teach about the law and the history of God's activity in the world. His sessions in the Temple prepared him for his future ministry. But notice that while Jesus had a passion for the things of God, he also loved and respected his parents.

Jesus' response to his mother may have surprised her. It even may have seemed rude. But Jesus didn't disrespect his parents. Once his parents found him, Jesus returned home with them. "Then he went down with them and came to Nazareth, and was obedient to them" (Luke 2:51). Jesus lived out the commandment "Honor your father and your mother" (Exodus 20:12).

Wrap it Up

When was the last time one of your parents said to you, "Child, why do you treat us this way?" As youth you are becoming more independent, but your parents may not be quite ready to let go. Before you walk out the door, they may need you to tell them exactly what your plans are. They need you to *want* to talk to them. When you get frustrated, remember that even Jesus had to be humble and respect, honor, and obey his parents.

So What?

- How would you describe your relationship with your parents right now?
- How will you model Jesus' respect and obedience in your relationship with your parents?

28. Joshua's Trust

The Point: to help youth trust God's plan even when others think they are crazy

The Scripture: "On the seventh day ... when the priests had blown the trumpets, Joshua said to the people, 'Shout! For the Lord has given you the city.' ... As soon as the people heard the sound of the trumpets, they raised a great shout, and the wall fell down flat" (Joshua 6:15, 16, 20).

Start Talking

The glass is half empty. The glass is half full. The task is doable. The task is impossible. ⌖ Your perspective on a situation can make all the difference. This is especially true when your perspective is aligned with God's. Joshua learned this truth at an early age.

Speak the Word

Thrust into the leadership circle with mentor and leader Moses, Joshua later assumed leadership as Moses' successor. Delivered from Egyptian slavery under Moses' leadership, Joshua showed himself to be a great warrior and leader. In fact, he was one of only two people who made it the entire journey from Egyptian slavery to life in the land promised by God.

At Rephidim (REF-ih-dim), where he defeated Amalek's army (Exodus 17:8-13), Joshua proved to be an able military leader. He was later part of a scouting party charged with surveying the land. Almost all of the other scouts expressed fear about going into and occupying the Promised Land. "We came to the land to which you sent us; it flows with milk and honey, and this is its fruit. Yet the people who live in the land are strong, and the towns are fortified and very large; and besides, we saw the descendants of Anak there" (Numbers 13:27-29). When the other spies were fearful and lacked confidence in their ability to go into the land God had promised them, Joshua, along with Caleb, encouraged the people to go forward. ⌖ He chose to adopt God's perspective on the situation and to follow God's plan.

The people in the Promised Land were numerous and powerful, but Joshua and Caleb insisted, "The land that we went through as spies is an exceedingly good land. If the Lord is pleased with us, he will bring us into this land and give it to us, a land that flows with milk and honey. Only, do not fear the people of the land, for they are no more than bread for us; their protection is removed from them, and the Lord is with us; do not fear them" (Numbers 14:7-10).

ᗤ Have you ever felt alone as you followed God? Joshua must have. I have. Most of the people who have answered God's call have experienced this feeling—even Jesus. God's plan is rarely the most popular. Let's be real. What man in his right mind would enter into a battle he was projected to lose?

As a child you probably sang or heard the song "Joshua Fit the Battle of Jericho." The LORD told Joshua that the walled city of Jericho had been given over to him. God instructed Joshua and seven priests to march around the city once a day for six days. On the seventh day they were to march around the city seven times, then blow trumpets and a ram's horn, and the city walls were supposed to fall down. Sounds crazy right? ᗤ But Joshua believed God. Joshua lived life by approaching things God's way. "On the seventh day . . . when the priests had blown the trumpets, Joshua said to the people, 'Shout! For the Lord has given you the city.' . . . As soon as the people heard the sound of the trumpets, they raised a great shout, and the wall fell down flat" (Joshua 6:15, 16, 20). ᗤ When faced with unfavorable odds, Joshua always trusted the LORD's instructions.

As a man of faith Joshua was favored by God. He accompanied Moses part of the way up Mt. Sinai when Moses had an encounter with God. Joshua (along with Caleb) was one of only two people who left Egyptian slavery who actually made it to the Promised Land. Not even Moses enjoyed that experience.

Wrap it Up

What life lessons we can learn from Joshua? He was obedient to God. He trusted God even when others thought his God-willed plan was insane. He had a great mentor in Moses who prepared him for future leadership and success. He trusted God's promises. By example Joshua encouraged an oppressed people to know that God not only loved them but also would work for their freedom, no matter how strong the opposition was.

Joshua saw the glass as half-full. He knew that God was in control; and his faith in God shaped his perspective on life. When you are stuck in a difficult situation, stop and think about your perspective. ⍟ Do you trust in God and believe that God can help you? Do you allow yourself to believe that there is no way out? You need to get this: God will deliver you. God's plan may seem unusual, but the God we serve is a deliverer. ⍟ When you allow your faith in God to shape your perspective, you won't be overcome by anything.

So What? ⍟

- ⍟ When have you had to check your perspective?
- ⍟ How does seeing God as a deliverer affect your relationship with God? How does it affect your outlook on life?
- ⍟ What will you do to gain the trust in God that Joshua had?

29. Ruth

The Point: to help youth come to know Ruth as a hero in
   faith

The Scripture: "Where you go, I will go; where you
   lodge, I will lodge; your people shall be my people, and
   your God my God. Where you die, I will die—there will I
   be buried. May the LORD do thus and so to me, and more as
   well, if even death parts me from you!" (Ruth 1:16-17).

Start Talking

The story of Ruth is unthinkable. Ruth, a widow, risked her life to
help her mother-in-law and in turn was blessed with a new
husband, land, and children. Ruth is in Jesus' lineage even though
she was not a Jew—pretty remarkable. Here are six reasons for
Ruth not to be in the lineage of Jesus:

   • She was considered a heathen.
   • She was a Gentile.
   • She was a Moabite, to be exact.
   • The Moabites did not worship the God of Abraham.
   • Marriage between Hebrews and Moabites was against
     Mosaic law.

Speak the Word

We encounter Ruth in Moab. Because of her ethnic background—
Ruth was a Moabite—no Hebrew male should have married her.
The Mosaic law forbade the union of a Hebrew man and a
Moabite woman. The people of Moab and Israel had a long and
troubled relationship. When the people of Israel traveled from
slavery in Egypt to the Promised Land, the Israelites camped in
Moab. The people of Moab were inhospitable (Numbers 22:1-6).
Nonetheless, the people of Israel began worshiping Baal of Peor,
a Moabite God. This idolatry incited God's anger.

Back to Ruth. Ruth had married Mahlon, the "sickly" son of
Naomi and her deceased husband, Elimelech (ih-LIM-uh-lek).
Naomi and Elimelech had traveled to Moab from Bethlehem, in

Israel, to escape a famine. Mahlon and his brother Chilion (KIL-ee-uhn) died leaving Ruth and her sister-in-law Orpah as widows. In the ancient near east, to be a widow without the aid of a male—whether a son, father, or husband—was to be in a dangerous situation. Women depended on men for their financial well-being. Ruth, Orpah, and Naomi faced peril. To ensure her survival, Naomi would have to return home to Bethlehem. If her foreign daughters followed her, they would most assuredly be subject to lives of poverty. While Orpah was loyal to Naomi, she took her mother-in-law's advice and stayed in Moab.

Ruth, on the other hand, would not leave Naomi. Even when Naomi encouraged Ruth to return to the security of her people and home, Ruth left her homeland, her culture, and her family and followed Naomi. Ruth told her mother-in-law, ☩ "Do not press me to leave you or to turn back from following you! Where you go, I will go; where you lodge, I will lodge; your people shall be my people, and your God my God. Where you die, I will die— there will I be buried. May the LORD do thus and so to me, and more as well, if even death parts me from you!" (Ruth 1:16-17).

Ruth's name itself speaks volumes about her disposition and role in this story. *Ruth* means "friend," "friend of God," and "something worth seeing." A woman who exhibited both external and internal beauty, Ruth befriended and loved her mother-in-law. Leaving the familiarity of family, culture, and location, she traveled to Bethlehem with Naomi. Ruth's selfless love ensured the survival of an elderly Hebrew woman who had become bitter after the death of her husband and sons. Naomi, whose name means "my joy, bliss" or "the pleasantness of Jehovah," referred to herself as "Mara" (meaning "bitter") after the loss of her husband and sons.

Going to Bethlehem with Naomi promised disaster for Ruth. Upon their arrival, the two of them were met with poverty. Ruth, in order to support the aged Naomi, had to glean fields for grain. God had instructed farmers not to harvest their entire fields, but to leave crops on the edges of the field for the poor—the widows and aliens—to pick so that they would be able to eat. Naomi was too old to glean for herself. Ruth's love and hard work sustained her mother-in-law.

As God's plan would have it, Ruth gleaned in the field owned by Boaz, a wealthy landowner and distant relative of Elimelech (Naomi's deceased husband). Boaz showed kindness to Ruth and

Scripture Talks: 50 Creative Messages for Youth

appreciation for her loyalty to Naomi. He bought the property owned by Naomi and Ruth's deceased husbands, Elimelech and Mahlon, and married Ruth, thus fulfilling the levirate law. According to levirate law, when a woman's husband died, the male next of kin—whether brother-in-law, cousin, or other relative—would marry her, provide for her, and have children with her to continue the lineage of the deceased.

Ruth's love for Naomi and her trust in God resulted in a turn of events that dramatically affected the biblical history. King David, "a man after God's own heart," and Israel's greatest king, was Ruth and Boaz's great grandson. Jesus, the Messiah, and reconciler of all humanity to God—both Jew and Gentile—descended from his forebears Ruth and Boaz. ⚬ This Gentile woman, this Moabite, exemplified God's desire for all people, despite their religious or ethnic backgrounds, to love and serve God and one another.

Wrap It Up

⚬ Ruth is a hero of faith because:

- She exhibited selfless love for another person—Naomi.
- She forfeited her faith in other gods to trust and serve the true God, the God of Naomi, Abraham, and Sarah.
- She became the great grandmother of King David.
- She became an ancestor of Jesus
- Her life foretells God's ultimate plan for both Jews and Gentiles to worship God and live in community with one another.

So What? ⚬

- Where do you find yourself in Ruth's story? Which character or situation do you most relate to?
- What can you learn from Ruth's courage and her willingness to put her family before her personal comfort?
- How does Ruth's story make you want to be a better friend, brother, or sister?

30. The Ten Commandments

The Point: to help youth understand and apply the Ten Commandments to their everyday lives

The Scripture: Exodus 20:1-17 and Deuteronomy 5:6-21 (Excerpts are printed throughout the talk.)

Start Talking

Every now and then I'll see a billboard that features one commandment and a "commentary" from God. One commentary that sticks out in my mind is "What part of no did you not understand?" While the billboards are generally simple reminders, it doesn't hurt to revisit the Ten Commandments and see how we're doing every now and then. So let's take a closer look.

Speak the Word

The Ten Commandments provided the foundation of loving, respectful behavior and relationships in the newly forming community of Israel after the people had left their lives of slavery in Egypt. After years of oppression and wandering in the wilderness, the people of Israel were being prepared for a new type of existence. At Mt. Sinai the people of Israel, who were "no people," would learn how live out their identity as "God's people."

The Ten Commandments, also known as the "Decalogue" (a Greek word that means, "the ten words from God"), gave the people guidelines for sustaining a holy and godly community, something they had never experienced before. The Commandments communicated God's desire for them and, ultimately, all people: love for God, their creator and redeemer, and love for their neighbors within—and, eventually, outside—their religious community. The Ten Commandments were not meant to be a list of strict directives to impede the freedom of God's beloved. Rather, they were meant to free God's people from oppression, harm, or robbery and to ensure justice for all.

The Commandments continue the covenant God made with Abraham and all of his future descendants. (See Genesis 17:9-10.)

Let's take a closer look at the commandments. Note that the first four commandments involve our relationship with God. The next six commandments involve our relationships with one another:

✝ **I.** "I am the Lord your God, who brought you out of the land of Egypt, out of the house of slavery; you shall have no gods before me" (Exodus 20:2-3). What's the big deal? you ask. While they were in Egypt and as they traveled to the Promised Land, the people of Israel were in contact with many peoples who worshiped many different gods. Each of these gods was consulted for a particular reason (for example, for the harvest or for safety). But God, the great I AM, was not the creation of human imagination and was to be worshiped and loved because God was faithful to the people of Israel. It was God who had delivered them from slavery. It was God alone whom they were to worship. Why worship some fake god anyway?

✝ **II.** "You shall not make for yourself an idol, whether in the form of anything that is in heaven above, or that is on earth beneath, or that is in the water under the earth" (Exodus 20:4). In other words, nothing can come before God. Idols don't have to be little statues that you bow down to; an idol can be anything that takes your mind off of God. What "idols" have you created or been tempted by? Your car? your friends? money? Anything that means more to us than God becomes our god.

✝ **III.** "You shall not make wrongful use of the name of the LORD your God, for the LORD will not acquit anyone who misuses his name" (Exodus 20:7). This is nothing to joke about. God is not a clown. God's name is a reflection of God's integrity and actions, and should therefore always be respected. When a person cusses or utters a curse word in conjunction with God's name, that person insults the very integrity of God. Think about the holiness of God's name next time you're tempted to misuse God's name or the next time you hear a friend do it.

✝ **IV.** "Remember the Sabbath day, and keep it holy. Six days you shall labor and do all your work. But the seventh day is a Sabbath to the LORD your God; you shall not do any work" (Exodus 20:8-10). If God took a day off to rest, what makes humans think we don't need one? God instituted the sabbath day so that humans could rest, worship, and pray. This gift points us to a reality that Americans and Westerners are now coming to terms with. We are realizing that we can't push the human body nonstop. Our bodies and spirits need time each week to rest and rejuvenate. Our society operates 24/7. Keeping up with this pace makes spending time with God in worship difficult. This commandment reminds us to stop what we're doing and spend quality time with God.

V. "Honor your father and your mother, so that your days may be long in the land that the LORD your God is giving you" (Exodus 20:12). Parents are God's representatives in the lives of their children, and are some of the only people who don't have to *earn* our respect. God calls us to respect and honor our parents—even if it requires a lot of prayer.

VI. "You shall not murder" (Exodus 20:13). All humans reflect the creativity of God. Even persons who are not in relationship with God are loved by God. All life is precious. No one has the right to take another person's life.

VII. "You shall not commit adultery" (Exodus 20:14). Promises, promises, blah, blah, blah. The truth is that God treasures marriages. When two people marry, they enter into covenant with one another. When one partner breaks the covenant, it results in heartache, distrust, and a broken relationship. God knows the pain that comes from adultery and wants wholeness for us.

VIII. "You shall not steal" (Exodus 20:15). Just look at some of the shows on television—*The O.C.* and *Cribs*. Man, these shows make you want to get what wealthy people have. But, truthfully, possessions don't define who you really are. To live in community you have to respect others' possessions. If you think you're doing well so far, think about the last time you cheated on an assignment. Cheating is stealing someone else's answer, you know.

IX. "You shall not bear false witness against your neighbor" (Exodus 20:16). Don't lie. Don't fib. Whether you tell a white lie or otherwise, lying is unacceptable to God. Lying reflects poorly on your honesty and integrity. Even if everyone else tells lies about you, don't tell lies about anyone else. Some people go through life thinking they are getting away with bearing false witness against others—gossip. But God sees and hears everything.

✞ **X.** "You shall not covet your neighbor's house; you shall not covet your neighbor's wife, or male or female slave, or ox, or donkey, or anything that belongs to your neighbor" (Exodus 20:17). In other words, don't even think about it! Keep your hands to yourself. Do not envy other people, regardless of what they have. God will bless you even if you don't get to have the luxuries that others have. Living in community means respecting others' possessions and relationships. When you covet, you fail to exercise your freedom of self-control. Breaking this commandment always results in broken relationships and ultimately results in your loss of freedom.

Wrap It Up

So how well are you keeping God's commandments? You probably haven't murdered anyone or committed adultery, but I challenge you to think about the idols that draw you away from God. Search your heart for the gods of the world that you put before God. Examine how you use God's name. Do you respect God's name and use it wisely? What about stealing, cheating, or wanting what others have?

These commandments are not meant to make us feel guilty. They are meant to free us. ✞ Boundaries, such as these laws, create a sense of freedom by protecting us from chaos. God doesn't expect us to follow these commandments on our own. God is always working in us through the Holy Spirit to make us aware of our sin, forgive us of these sins, and free us to live more devoted lives as disciples.

So What? ✞

- ⟡ Which commandment do you struggle with the most?
- ⟡ What is God saying to you now about living out these commandments?
- ⟡ How will you live differently if you understand the Ten Commandments as a ticket to freedom?

David Stewart
is a small town
Mississippi boy with a huge
heart. His creativity opens
doors and makes church a
welcoming place for all, no matter
who and no matter what. For the
past 19 years he has worked with
groups averaging between 13 and
400 students each week. He is an
influential minister and a loving friend.

Dave is one of those youth pastors
who can grow a youth group from
one to 100 in no time at all. He is a
visionary in youth ministry and an
awesome speaker. His talks all
come from tried and tested
programs that he has led over
the past ten years. All you
need to do with them is run
them through your filter
and add your own
stories.

31. Worship: It's All About Jesus

The Point: to help youth discover a passion for worship

The Scripture: "David danced before the Lord with all his might" (2 Samuel 6:14).

Recommended Resource

For a complete program based on this talk, see *Combos: Six Month-Long Themes With the Works* (Abingdon Press, 2004; ISBN 0687740029)

Start Talking

☙ Did you know that we were created to worship? It's true! That's why it is so easy for us to worship almost anyone or anything—athletes, actors, possessions, and yes, even ourselves. Think about big sporting events. When a favorite baseball player hits a home run, fans go crazy—screaming, jumping, giving high-fives, making so much noise that you can't hear yourself think. Football stadiums fill with people and paraphernalia—replica jerseys, programs, food, bands, cheerleaders, dance teams. The announcer says, "It's football time!" and 108,000 people go nuts.

Around here things can get pretty exciting too. Youth all over the place—food, games, small groups, free stuff, excitement. Not much different from a football game. So what makes us different? ☙ What's our reason for being here?

Are you here just to hang out with your friends? That's OK. Are you here because have your eye on a cute girl or guy? That's kind of OK. Are you here to jump up and down during the songs and get some exercise? There are plenty of reasons to be here. ☙ But our main reason for coming should be to meet with God.

Speak the Word

To meet God we need to put aside distractions and focus on what's really important. We go through life busy, caught up in our agendas, and filled with worry; we wonder what certain people think about us; we realize that we are angry with certain other people; and so on. We bring all of that baggage with us and miss out on the blessings of worship. We just go through the motions.

Have you ever been sitting in worship—this might be happening to you right now—when your mind wanders off, and, eventually, when you come back to reality, you have no clue what is going on? Compare that experience to that of youth who know why they're here. They want to meet God. They can set aside distractions and sing every song like it's a prayer or a celebration. They dance!

Worship expresses our love for God; it renews our spirits; it is practice for eternity; it is how we live. Everything we do should be worship. ✝ Everything we do should make God smile.

✝ Listen to this story from the Old Testament: "When King David brought the the ark of the LORD back to Jerusalem, everyone was thrilled. David took off all of his clothes and, wearing only a linen cloth, danced for the LORD with all his might. He and his people celebrated by shouting and blowing horns.

"David's wife, Michal, looked out the window and saw the celebration. When she saw David jumping around and dancing for the LORD, she was disgusted.

"Once, the ark had been placed inside the tent that David had set up for it, David made sacrifices and blessed his people in the name of the LORD. He gave everyone in the crowd bread, meat, and some raisins; and they went home to celebrate some more.

"When David went home to bless his family, he was met by Michal. She said, 'You were *great* today! You acted like a crazy old man, dancing around half-naked.' David replied, 'I was celebrating to honor God.' " (Adapted from 2 Samuel 6:12-22.)

David danced! He didn't care what people thought of him. Worshiping God was his passion. It should be ours as well.

Wrap It Up

What keeps us from dancing? Would we worship differently if God, the Creator, appeared right here in front of us? What if there were no jumping, no screaming, no lights, no music, no distractions? ✝ If it were just you and God, would you dance?

So What? ✝

- ❧ What keeps you from all-out worship?
- ❧ What is your favorite way to worship God?
- ❧ What would cause you to dance with the joy and energy that David had?

Scripture Talks: 50 Creative Messages for Youth

32. Hey, Let's Play!

The Point: to help youth play the game of life as fully devoted followers of Christ

The Scripture: "His master replied, 'Well done, good and faithful servant! You have been faithful with a few things; I will put you in charge of many things. Come and share your master's happiness!'" (Matthew 25:23, NIV).

Start Talking

Remember when you were kids and you spent hours pretending to be Power Rangers™ or Teenage Mutant Ninja Turtles®?

One of the best imagination games involved lying in the grass and looking up at the sky. You would wait for a cloud to float by, then tell what you thought the cloud looked like. Life was so simple.

And you know, Legos™ always fit together. When we were kids school was about smiley faces, addition, and spelling. Life was one long, fun recess.

As we grew up, recess turned into work. Alice left Wonderland, and the bogeyman entered our dreams. Cops and robbers turned into spies and terrorists. Now it's hard to know who the bad guys really are.

And, the rage today? Reality games? What do we win? Relationships that are shallow and dysfunctional or reduced to a big pot of cash?

The real games now are on CNN: "The Showdown With Iraq" and "The Tension With North Korea." To some the news all seems like a big video game, but the game pieces are real bombs and real people. Makes you wonder if anybody really wins.

We've sure come a long way from hopscotch. Life has changed. It's easy to be cynical, even depressed. Living with the hand we've been dealt can be difficult, especially when there are so many wild cards.

High School graduation and college are on the horizon for most of you. In the coming years your life will change in significant ways. ✄ Life is about change and how we respond to change.

Speak the Word

Let's talk for a minute about The Game of Life®. How to play: Spin the wheel; go to school; get a job; make as much money as you can; get married; have some kids; and hopefully climb the ladder of success to Millionaire Acres, avoiding The Poor House at all costs. [If you own this game, use the game board and pieces to demonstrate the different steps.]

Now listen up! This might shock some of you, but I really do hope that some of you become very, very rich! Not so you can impress people by having the biggest and best toys, but so that you can invest in people, so that you can invest in ministries like this that change the lives of youth.

The truth is that you are already playing the game of life. ✄ Some of your decisions today will affect all of your tomorrows. So here's some advice and a question to consider:

Don't look at today! Look toward the end. Think about when the game is over. What do you want to be known for? What do you want people to remember about you? Whom did you love? Who loved you? In whom did you invest your life? ✄ When the game is over, and you are standing before God, what do you want God to say to you?

Your answers to these questions can be your trump cards in your game of life, because your answers should affect how you live each day. Your answers can help you respond to changes in life even when it seems like winning the game will be very difficult.

Your answers will also help you form a personal "mission statement." I challenge you to make writing a mission statement a priority this week. Come up with a short phrase that summarizes your answers. Stick a copy on your bathroom mirror. Memorize it. Commit to making your mission statement a part of everyday.

If you want to be known as friendly, be the best friend you can each day. If you want to be known as giving, give and expect nothing in return. ⚲ If you want to be known as loving or forgiving or as a servant, love the way God loves, forgive the way God forgives, and do your best to imitate the life of Jesus.

Take responsibility for your life. Be careful about what habits you pick up. They can make or break you. Give yourself regular attitude checks. Take time to renew yourself daily. Know that some things are beyond your control. Don't beat yourself up. Listen more than you speak.

You've seen bumper stickers that say, "Life Is Short. Pray Hard." That is no joke! Write a few lines in a journal each night. Read a verse from the Book of Proverbs each day. Be courageous and confident in who you are. Work with others and be cooperative. And make sure you have some cheerleaders. ⚲ Helen Keller said, "Alone we can do so little, together we can do so much."

Wrap It Up

Our mission here—our project—is to become passionate followers of Jesus Christ. This is not a concert. This is not a show. This is about doing what it takes to share the true message of life.

If you are here for the first time and you are looking for a place to get involved and make a difference, join us in the game.

I pray that each of you will decide to live your lives in such a way that, when the game is over and you stand before God, God will be able to say to you, "Well done passionate follower! Welcome home!"

⚲ Our mission is to change the world. So hey, let's play!

So What? ⚲

- 🗨 What do you want to be known for?
- 🗨 How can we invite others into God's game of abundant life?
- 🗨 Why is working together with others so important in the game of life?

33. God's Amazing Offer

The Point: to help youth unload all of the baggage they carry around into the forgiving, loving arms of Christ

The Scripture: "God's love has been poured into our hearts through the Holy Spirit that has been given to us. For while we were still weak, at the right time Christ died for the ungodly" (Romans 5:5-6).

Start Talking

[Tell a story about a ridiculous infomercial you have seen or about a rumor or offer that seems too good to be true.]

Speak the Word

Read aloud Romans 5:12-21.

You know the story of how Adam landed us in the dilemma we're in. His sin broke our relationship with God and with everything and everyone else. But the extent of this brokenness was not clear until God spelled it out in detail to Moses. So death—this huge abyss separating us from God—dominated the landscape from Adam until Moses. Even those who didn't disobey a specific command of God as Adam did, still had to experience the termination of life, and the separation from God. But Adam, who got us into this, also points ahead to the One who would ultimately get us out of it. Yet the rescuing gift is not exactly parallel to the death-dealing sin.

If one man's sin throws crowds of people into the dead-end abyss of separation from God, just think of what God's gift of Jesus Christ will do! There's no comparison between Adam's death-dealing sin and God's generous, life-giving gift. The verdict on Adam's sin was the death sentence; the verdict on the many sins that have followed was a wonderful life sentence. ✌ If death got the upper hand through one man's wrongdoing, can you imagine the breathtaking recovery of life, this wildly extravagant life-gift, this grand setting-everything-right, that the one man Jesus Christ provides?

All sorts of things weigh us down. Some are trivial: our haircuts, the labels on our clothes, popularity, what others say about us. Some are almost debilitating: guilt, doubt, the pain of loss, the inability to forgive others and ourselves. Many possessions and habits weigh us down by making us their slaves, leaving us with what seems to be only one choice—changing our notion of right and wrong. ✍ What is it in your backpack that is weighing you down?

Here's a truth for you to hold onto with both hands: ✍ You are not what you do! This statement will be difficult to swallow if you feel your identity comes from something you do. For example, "I'm a football player," "I'm a cheerleader," "I'm a . . . whatever." But for others this statement is liberating. It says that you are not a loser, moron, failure, liar, cheater, thief, or druggie. Labels are just extra weight you don't need to carry. And you shouldn't force others to carry excess weight either. ✍ You see, our true identities come from the Creator, our Heavenly Father who claims us as children. This is good news. We are God's children!

Truth: God created us and wants to have a loving relationship with us. Sin created a divide between us and God. God is over there and we are over here. No matter how good we are we cannot get over there. No matter how much we sacrifice, how many Bible verses we memorize, how many spiritual practices we master, there is no way we can bridge that great divide. But God never gave up on the relationship. God sent Jesus to live as we live, to die for our sins, and to restore our relationships with God.

Story Illustration
(Here's my story, but you can tell a better one of your own.)

Have you ever carried something really heavy a long way? When I was younger, I was a Boy Scout. Our troop had an annual tradition: Each year, a group would be selected to go on a 20-mile hike. Now, I know what you're thinking: "I could never hike 20 miles!" But, there was an incentive: a medal! Every boy who finished the hike got a medal to wear on his uniform, and I wanted one of those medals! It was really important to me. The day came for the hike, and I was so excited! But I quickly discovered a problem I had not previously considered: Twenty miles! And there was this backpack—a very heavy backpack! During the hike I lost sight of the goal. The medal seemed so much less important than my aching feet and back. I wondered what my mother had put in the backpack. When we stopped for a rest, I started digging through it. (Three pairs of underwear for a two-day trip? for a middle school boy?) The deeper I dug, the more I realized how many things in that backpack I did not need.

Through Jesus, God returned to us our true identities. God says, "Believe and I will forgive your sins. I will forget them. I will be with you. I will change you from the inside out." You will be tempted. You will fail and miss the mark. But, it's no longer just "you versus sin." It can be "you and God versus sin."

Wrap It Up

It is possible to break bad habits. It is possible to get rid of the baggage that weighs you down. It is possible to become a new person. All you have to do is grasp with both hands this wildly extravagant life-gift, this grand "setting-everything-right" that Jesus Christ provides.

Read aloud Romans 5:5 again.

If you would like to empty your backpack, you can! You can even leave it here! You don't even have to pick it up and take it home. God wants you to know the truth. You are God's child. God loves you. And, no matter what you've done, God will forgive you.

So What?

- What does it mean to you that God created a way to be in relationship with you?
- What is in your backpack that you need to get rid of?
- What is God saying to you right now about starting over?

34. Back to the Dump

The Point: to help students leave their failures at the dump and move on in Christ

The Scripture: "He began to curse, and he swore an oath, 'I do not know this man you are talking about' " (Mark 14:71).

Start Talking

Show the clip from *O Brother, Where Art Thou*.

Speak the Word

Peter was a disciple. He walked with Jesus for three years. But when it came time for Peter to prove himself, he denied Jesus three times. He failed the test. What happened to Peter happens to all of us. We encounter Christ. We say "the prayer." We give our lives to God, and then we fail, we mess up, we sin. We get down on ourselves and wonder if being a good Christian is impossible.

Maybe our problem is that we've never been taught how to handle failure. Our culture is based on performance, on winning. Sure we are told to be "good sports"; but I'll admit that I sometimes have trouble being a "good sport," and I'm not even an athlete. Have you ever heard a coach or teacher say, "Today, I'm going to teach you how to fail correctly." Of course not! We don't like to talk about our weaknesses; and we definitely don't want others pointing out our shortcomings. We even "talk up" ourselves to make us appear to be more than we really are. Just read some of the personal ads on the Internet—tall, dark, handsome, funny, rich. Yeah, right!

Here's the truth. ✌ Life is about success *and* failure. And how we respond to both determines how we will live. Take Michael Jordan, for example. He was probably the greatest basketball

Movie idea

O Brother, Where Art Thou

Show the baptism scene and talk about the how baptism symbolizes throwing away our "junk."

Before showing the clip, see the note on permissions on page 175.

player of all time. But, as a sophomore, he was cut from his high school team.

[Draw a line in the air with your finger.] Let's say this line represents the expectations—ours and others'—that we are asked to live up to. [Draw another line with your finger well below the first line.] This line represents where we are now. The gap between the two lines represents disappointment. We get disappointed when we fail to live up to our expectations or the expectations of others. The more failure we experience, the wider the gap.

Many people respond to failure in one of four ways. � They "blow up," "cover up," "speed up," or "give up." Some people "blow up"—they blame everybody, cuss, scream, and throw things. Many of us try to "cover up" our failures as quickly as possible. Some people "speed up"—they work harder, longer, and faster when they experience failure. And some people simply "give up." But successful athletic teams watch hours of game film to learn from their past mistakes, to try to find new ways of attacking their problems, to narrow the gap between reality and expectation.

Have you ever been called a failure? Turn to a neighbor and tell him or her, ⏝ "You are going to fail!" Uncomfortable, eh? But failure is not the enemy. Failure can actually teach more than winning can. It's not as fun; that's for sure. Now reassure your neighbors, and tell them, ⏝ "Failure is an event, it is not who we are!"

Now I'm going to say something that even I find scary. Ready? We must allow each other to fail, because, truthfully, we all will. We must allow each other to fail. But we shouldn't judge one another. ⏝ Our job is to pick up one another when we fail.

Let's go back to the dump and leave our failures there. We've said the prayer. We've given our lives to God. Shouldn't we be perfect by now? No! The Bible is full of people who loved God, but committed some atrocious sins. Here's a strange thing about God: God gives us free will—the freedom to choose, the freedom to mess up, the freedom to sin. God did not give us free will, knowing that we would mess up, so that God could have reasons to strike us dead with lightning. ⏝ Instead, God gave us free will so that we could *choose* to worship God, so that we could *choose* to believe, *choose* to follow, and *choose* to love. God knows that

Scripture Talks: 50 Creative Messages for Youth

at some point every one of us will be standing in the middle of a mess wondering what happened. God knows that accidents will happen. God knows our bad habits and our "pet" sins. No matter how hard we try, we won't be perfect. We need help. By ourselves we can never be good enough for God. Our failings point to our need for a Savior.

Truth: Jesus died for our mistakes, failures, and sins—past, present, and future! The Bible says that God remembers them no more. Hear this! ✆ When God looks at us, God sees beloved children. If God sees us as beloved children, then we shouldn't beat ourselves up when we fail to be the Christians we think we should be. Reality [draw a line in the air with your finger]. Expectation [draw a second line, higher than the first]. Jesus died to bridge the disappointment gap—to make it possible for us to connect with God. If you are caught in a circle of failure, these two truths can liberate you: Jesus died for you and God claims you as God's own child. Have faith. Know who you are. When you fall, get up and try again. You can gain strength from each failure. ✆ Don't give up!

Wrap It Up

Here's a suggestion that will help you grow from failure: Ask a friend to walk alongside you on your spiritual journey. Promise each other that you will always be honest and open about what is going on in your lives. Be transparent to each other. Share your struggles. Keep each other from beating yourselves up. Give your friend the power to call the "junk" in your life "junk." Pray with each other. And, when your friend fails, messes up, sins, falls, be the first to run to your friend and help him or her up. Peter had denied Jesus three times. But after Jesus was raised from the dead, he and Peter had an interesting conversation. Jesus asked Peter three times, "Do you love me?" Each time, Peter said yes. (See John 21:15-19.) Jesus picked him up. That's our job today: to pick up one another and walk away from the dump of failure together!

So What? ✆

- What "junk" do you need to leave behind?
- How do you deal with failure? What have you learned from failure?
- Who will be your partner as you leave your failures at the dump and follow Christ?

35. Being Light

The Point: to help youth shine Christ's light into the world

Story idea

(Here is my story; tell a similar story of your own.)

When I was younger, I was terrified of the dark. Terrified with a capital "T." I grew up on a farm. At night, farms have the strangest noises: Cows sound like ghosts; dumb dogs bark at anything and everything. One of my chores was to go to the storage house in the back yard to get food out of the freezer for supper. I tried to be an obedient son, but there was one problem: The light from the house did not reach all the way to the building where the freezer was! I would walk to the edge of the light, listen cautiously, and strain to see through the darkness. Then I would carefully and quickly walk to the freezer and throw open the door so that the light would come on. And when I had found what I had been sent to get, I would slam the freezer door shut and run as fast as my two legs could carry me back to the light.

The Scripture

"In the beginning God created the heavens and the earth. The earth was barren, with no form of life; it was under a roaring ocean covered with darkness. But the Spirit of God was moving over the water. God said, 'I command light to shine!' And light started shining. God looked at the light and saw that it was good. He separated light from darkness and named the light 'Day' and the darkness 'Night.' Evening came and then morning—that was the first day" (Genesis 1:1-5, CEV).

Start Talking

Studies show that we need natural light to remain healthy. Have you ever noticed that people get depressed during the winter months when there's less daylight? This condition is called Seasonal Affective Disorder. The days get shorter and are usually cloudy and the cold keeps us inside. Our bodies miss the sunlight. Imagine living in Barrow, Alaska, where it stays dark for two months!

Speak the Word

I love Christmas, because it is a time when God says again, "Let there be light!" Hear this story from Luke:

⍟ "That night in the fields near Bethlehem some shepherds were guarding their sheep. All at once an angel come down to them from the Lord, and the brightness of the Lord's glory flashed around them. The shepherds were frightened. But, the angel said, 'Don't be afraid! I have good news for you, which will make everyone happy. This very day in King David's hometown a Savior was born for you. He is Christ the Lord' " (Luke 2:8-11, CEV).

Maybe this story will help us better understand this issue: A family took a cave tour deep into the earth. When they arrived in a large open space, they were told to sit down and be very quiet. The tour guide told them that he was going to turn out the lights so that they could experience total darkness. If I were in their situation, I would start feeling very uneasy! The youngest boy in the family grabbed his older brother's hand, leaned over, and said, "I'm scared." The older brother squeezed the boy's hand and said, "Don't worry! Someone knows where the light switch is."

The world is asking, ⍟ "Does anyone know where the light switch is?" People are looking for light in all kinds of places— crystals, drugs, sex, material possessions, athletics, new age groups, self-help books, you name it!

We all experience darkness: illness, death, separation and divorce, tragedy. We are often trapped by poor decisions. Too often our faith is based on feelings—"How was *my* day?" But we need to base our faith on what God has done for us. ⍟ When Jesus was born, God said again, "Let there be light," and wise men followed God's star. When Jesus was crucified, darkness covered the earth. But on Sunday morning, when Jesus was resurrected, an angel came down from heaven and rolled away the stone of the sealed tomb. According to Matthew, "The angel looked as bright as lightning, and his clothes were white as snow" (Matthew 28:3, CEV). The soldiers guarding the tomb shook with fear and fell down as though they had died. "The angel said to the women, 'Don't be afraid! I know you are looking for Jesus, who was nailed to the cross. He isn't here! God raised him to life, just as Jesus said he would. Come, see the place where his body was lying. Now hurry! Tell his disciples that he has been raised to life' " (Matthew 28:5-7, CEV).

Here's the light switch! Who will turn on the lights?

⍟ Jesus says in Matthew, "You are like light for the whole world. A city built on top of a hill cannot be hidden, and no one would light a lamp and put it under a clay pot. A lamp is placed on a lamp stand, where it can give light to everyone in the house. Make your light shine, so that others will see the good that you do and will praise your Father in heaven" (Matthew 5:14-16, CEV).

Wrap It Up

We not only know how to turn the lights on, but, as Christians, we are called to *be* light to the world. We are to be peacemakers. We are to be givers. We are to feed, house, clothe, visit, forgive, and love. We are called to be different. Someone recently told me, "There's no difference between Christians and non-Christians. Whatever happens out there is going to happen in here." Probably true, but definitely sad. We must be different. Some places are really dark and scary! The military has developed special goggles that allow soldiers to see in the dark. Even in the darkest spaces, the lenses collect what little light there is and concentrate it so that the person wearing the goggles can see. That's our job! We've got to help others see! We've got to be the light in the darkest situations.

So What?

- How does Christ's light shine through you?
- What will you do to turn the lights on in your life?
- How will you be a light to the world?

Scripture Talks: 50 Creative Messages for Youth

36: Success

The Point: to help youth judge success in their lives through God's eyes

The Scripture: " 'For this son of mine was dead and is alive again; he was lost and is found.' So they began to celebrate" (Luke 15:24).

Start Talking

You've probably heard the parable of the prodigal son a million times. But, let's look closer at this story. The prodigal son had everything: lots of money, freedom, friends, women. He lived the "good life." Even I admit that his lifestyle sounds very attractive. He had found success, admiration, and popularity. We eat that stuff up, don't we?

Merriam-Webster's Collegiate Dictionary defines pride as "a reasonable or justifiable self-respect." Nothing is wrong with that. Everyone should set high goals and do their best to achieve these goals. Confidence and self-esteem are major concerns for most people. But it's amazing where our self-esteem sometimes comes from: the people we hang out with, the car we drive, the SAT score we get, our physical appearance, the person we date, our job. We will do whatever it takes to look good and feel good! But it's amazing how quickly circumstances change and feelings fade.

Truthfully, many of us live with a false sense of security about who we are. We've been conditioned to want the latest clothes, the sleekest car, the biggest house. We love quick solutions, self-help books, and easy answers. We get implants, reductions, and lifts. A youth recently told me, "A 1300 not only gets me into good

Story idea

Tell about big dream of yours that seems unattainable. Here's mine: One of my fantasies is to run in the New York Marathon. I know it's crazy! It's easy to see that I'm not a runner! I don't even like running! But what a rush it would be to finish! Even if I were last, I could always say that I ran the New York Marathon. We all want something to hold on to and be proud of.

schools, that 1300 defines me." It's sad but true. These things give us identity. They define us. ⊘ They mean we are accepted by somebody. We become what we do and value—athlete, brain, rich girl, bad boy. We fit in somewhere! We are successful! As long as we look the look, talk the talk, and walk the walk.

Speak the Word

The prodigal son had it all until a famine swept through the land and his lifestyle caught up with him. He lost his money! his status! his friends! everything! He had to take the worst job around: feeding pigs. He was so desperate that he would have eaten what the pigs ate. Talk about a blow to your self-esteem. From top to bottom just like that! He was alone.

What happened to the prodigal son happens to all of us. Things are going great . . . then BAM! Reality sets in. The fantasy is over. Friends reject you. Your parents split up. You move. Somebody new enters your circle of friends. Your looks fade. You lose. You think life is over.

Some of my favorite worship songs talk about wanting to be broken, but what kind of prayer is that? To be broken? I don't want to be broken. I want to look good. I want people to think I've got it all together. ⊘ Should we really pray for brokenness?

When life is going well, we are often tempted to think that we don't need God. I bet we all have days when we rarely think about God at all. But once something goes wrong it's, "Oh, Lord please help me!" or "Please, Lord, fix this!" God is reduced to aspirin—an escape from pain.

Brokenness. It's why Jesus had to die. If we could reach perfection or be truly successful on our own, we wouldn't need a Savior. Brokenness. I know it sounds strange. I mean we are talking about success aren't we? Christ says that whenever we are weak, then we are strong. ⊘ God is powerful in our brokenness, in our weakness. Brokenness and success: It's a strange combination. But, truthfully, God sees success as more than just a feeling or an accomplishment. Success is more than just convincing yourself and others that you're special. It's not about how good you are or how powerful you become. ⊘ Success in God's eyes is not about getting it right. You won't. You can't!

Wrap It Up

Success in God's eyes is about a relationship. God the Father, like the father in the story, waits. All the son did was return home. The father was waiting. The son was accepted by his father simply because he was the son.

Do you want to know how to be sure God that is always with you? Ask yourself nagging questions, such as, "Will I ever?" or "What's wrong with me?" or "Why can't I?" If you listen closely, you will hear God answer, "I love you! You are my child! I will never let you go!"

⌘ How is your relationship with the Father? If you claim to be Christ's follower, how passionate are you about your relationship with Christ? If you are not a follower, do you feel a void in your life? as though you just aren't complete or happy? like you've tried everything and the feeling never lasts? You are broken. Right now I invite you to take steps toward home. You want the relationship, the love, and the acceptance. Come, now! You will find God, the Father, running out to meet you with arms open wide.

So What? ⌘

- Where do you see yourself in the parable of the prodigal son?
- What is God saying to you right now about success?
- How does someone's life change when he or she is restored and in a relationship with God?

Sheet I am —
what we are in Christ

37. This Is Your Life, Part 1

List of what

The Point: to help youth see themselves and others as God sees them

The Scripture: "Truly I tell you, just as you did it to one of the least of these who are members of my family, you did it to me" (Matthew 25:40).

Roll Play
- *Jock*
- *Smart Kid*
- *Premadonna*

Start Talking → *Act out Rolls*
Have students

Question: When people look at you what do they see? Boy or girl, jock or brain (like you can't be both), Abercrombie and Fitch model material or JC Penny model material? When people look at you what do they see? It's a scary question when you really think about it. I know it's a scary question when *I* think about it.

Speak the Word

When people look at you what do they see? Let me tell you a story: A church had a service each Thursday that was primarily for homeless people. One cold night, during "joys and concerns," a man said that he was concerned about his health. Homelessness and bitter cold don't go well together. This man was particularly concerned because he had no shoes. This sent the church staff into "fix-it mode." A frantic search began. There were no shoes in the lost and found; there were no shoes in the donation box; there were no shoes anywhere. Finally, another homeless man said, "Here! Take my shoes. I have another pair under the bridge."

God Sees
perfect

Use A mirror

WOW! No one else had thought of donating their own shoes. All the people who had ten or more pairs of shoes at home didn't think to give this man a pair of their own shoes. But this homeless guy, living out his faith, gave his shoes away.

(*Talk continued on page 130.*)

- Acting out Parts
- Sheet of I am's
- Scripture

Story Illustrations

(Use your own examples, or say that you heard these from a friend).

Slow drivers are one of my pet peeves. They make me so mad! The speed limit is 45 and they're driving slower than a golf cart, talking on their phone. They drive me crazy!

Here's another example of my "dark side": People in front of me at grocery store. I have 13 items; they have 500. They can't decide on paper or plastic. They always have a handful of coupons, and of course they have to count out correct change down to the penny.

I'm glad people can't read my mind. One day I was doing yard work with a friend. We went to the recycle center to get free mulch. A man had let me borrow his old truck. While we were piling the mulch into the back of the truck, I decided that I was ready to find an ATM and go to the K-Mart garden center—where they sell mulch in bags.

Alas, we finally filled the truck. But as I got ready to go, I noticed, among the many other people filling their trucks, an older guy struggling to shovel the mulch. I stood there thinking, "I hope this guy doesn't have a heart attack." Oh well, my "dark side" told me it was time to go. But, to my surprise, my friend yelled to the old man, "Hey, you want some help?" I was furious! I was like, "Hey! Let's go! We've got work to do. Let that guy go to K-Mart." But I picked up the pitch fork and helped fill the man's truck. When we had finished, I thought, "Wow! That's what Christianity is all about: helping an old man whom we don't even know fill his truck with mulch."

Later on, when we'd finished our yard work, my friend got out the vacuum, the hose, the glass cleaner, and the car wax and started cleaning the old truck we'd borrowed. I was thinking we'd fill it with gas and take it back. He was thinking we should return the truck in better condition than it was in when we picked it up. I don't know if my friend was thinking about doing "the Christian thing to do," but he taught me a lot about being a Christian that day.

Story idea

(Use a similar story, or say you heard this one from a friend.)

One of my favorite homeless people was Carol. She didn't know her last name. She was a walking rainbow of rags who slept on the bench outside our sanctuary. We called her our security guard. I felt sorry for her for the longest time. But, eventually she became part of the landscape. She became invisible. That is, until I took a class at a local seminary. I was assigned to write a paper on Jesus as a woman. (I was the only man in the class.) I looked at pictures of women teaching children, feeding people, even being crucified. Needless to say, I struggled with the assignment. Jesus as a woman? No way! But then a Scripture came to mind: Matthew 25:31-46. Judgment, separation, sheep, goats, blessed, cursed, did good things, didn't do good things ... I had heard this story a million times, but this time I really heard it. When you do things for others, especially when you know they can't repay you, you do them for Jesus. So I went and sat with Carol for about three hours. I listened to her simple, yet beautiful, view of life. We shared a Diet Coke® and some cookies. From that day on, Carol was no longer invisible. She was Jesus. So, I wrote my paper. Carol: Jesus As a Woman.

Wrap it Up

When people look at you what do you see? When you look at others what do you see? We are so often separated by our differences—race, gender, nationality, economic status. These things shouldn't matter! It's no wonder people look at the church and say, "Whatever! You say you believe in Jesus, but your lives don't reflect your beliefs." We must remember that we are all children of God, equal in grace. ✝ Let's commit to living what we say we believe, loving God above all else, loving ourselves as God loves us, and loving others in the same way.

So What? ✝

- Who are the "least of these" in our world?
- What do people see when they look at you?
- How can you see God in the faces of others?

38. This Is Your Life, Part 2

The Point: to help youth recognize the hold the world has on them and challenge them to make their lives count for Christ

The Scripture: "You are the light of the world. A city built on a hill cannot be hid. No one after lighting a lamp puts it under the bushel basket, but on the lampstand, and it gives light to all in the house. In the same way, let your light shine before others, so that they may see your good works and give glory to your Father in heaven" (Matthew 5:14-16).

Start Talking

My chemistry and biology teachers began the school year by saying, "There are two bottles on your table that you should not touch." One had white stuff in it that would pop, fizz, and smoke when it was mixed with water. It was too cool! I couldn't wait until the teacher wasn't looking so that I could try it. The other bottle contained sulfuric acid, which will eat right through you. I wondered, "Why are these bottles even on the table? You can't just tell kids not to mess with stuff that is cool and dangerous."

One day, we had to dissect frogs. Now these frogs arrived alive, and you had to kill your frog before dissecting it. There were two ways to kill your frog. The angry-heavy-metal-boy method, called "pithing" which involved taking a probe (a small stick with a sharp needle), holding the frog tightly, and stabbing the frog in the head to scramble its little brain.

The second option was more merciful. It involved putting the frog in a container of water, putting a Bunsen burner under the container, and slowly heating the water. The frog died a slow, painless death in a froggy hot tub. I felt that this option was the more Christian of the two (and it enabled you to eat the frog when you were done). Life is a lot like killing frogs. Sometimes we feel scrambled. But most of the time things slowly eat away at us and wear us down.

Speak the Word

Think of it this way: Society has taken you and your Christian faith, put you in warm, comfortable water, and is turning up the heat. I know that it's not easy to be a Christian at school. Many students have trouble maintaining their integrity and commitment to Christ. In fact, being a Christian can be extremely difficult for everyone—you, the volunteers and other adults in the room, your parents, and myself. It's as if some invisible force seeks to divert us from our walk with Christ. It's one thing to come to youth group—to sing, pray, laugh, dance, cry, quiet your heart, listen to God. It's quite another to express your faith during first period, when you're out on a date, or when you're taking a test knowing that everyone else is cheating. Being a Christian here is much easier than being a Christian outside these walls.

Imagine this conversation: I'm talking to someone your age. He says that he was a Christian, but that he has drifted and gotten sucked into drinking, sex, and drugs. He says that he knows these things are wrong. So I ask him, "How did you get involved with these things?" and "Why don't you stop?" He says, "It's easier to relate to people through drugs and sex than to be honest, truthful, and Christian." He continues, "My Christian friends who are doing what I'm doing think I'm cool. My Christian friends who aren't doing what I'm doing don't want anything to do with me."

Two things: 1) If you surround yourself only with good, Christian friends, you have *little* chance of bringing someone to Christ. 2) If you aren't living your beliefs outside these walls, you have *no* chance of bringing someone to Christ. The youth I'm talking to continues, "It's hard to be a Christian at school and on weekends. We're all climbing ladders: to improve our social status, to improve our grade point averages, to accomplish something. Everybody is climbing, and the pressure is tremendous. Christianity takes too much work. I come to church for a break, but people climb ladders here too."

It's easy to be a believer. It's hard to live out your beliefs! Sometimes we get so busy that we hardly think of God. Other things demand our attention—now! Christianity can wait, right? Committing to living our faith can be scary. When the church asks for more commitment, participation usually drops. If the church plans events that are fun and require little effort, attendance sky-rockets.

Here's a question for you: How true are you to your commitment to Christ? Right now I want us as a group and as individuals to be committed. Remember: have a project and the passion to match it. If you have made a commitment to Christ, you have a project! If you are committed to that commitment, you have passion! ✧ Passion leads to allegiance! Allegiance leads to integrity!

Wrap it Up

The American Heritage Dictionary defines *integrity* as, "The quality or condition of being whole or undivided." Integrity means having enough character to live up to what we believe. We must be wholly devoted to God. God must be priority #1. I'll admit that it sometimes seems impossible to make God the top priority. I often find myself in warm, comfortable water that is slowly getting hotter.

Paul describes himself as a "captive to the law of sin" (Romans 7:23). Yet he started churches throughout the Roman world and wrote many of the letters found in the New Testament. He was a sinner leading sinners. So let's look at it this way: Hold up one finger. This finger represents your commitment to Christ. Now think of everything else in your life: school, family, friends, athletics, arts, job. Which of these is priority #1 in your life? Is your relationship with Christ first? How about your social life or dating life? When your friends walk in the front door, do you push God out the back door?

The world is crying out for and dying to see Christians live out what we say we believe. Do you think anyone has ever looked at your life and said, "Forget this religion thing! It doesn't really mean anything to the people who say they believe it." When people look at our youth ministry, what do they see? Do they see people who love, forgive, encourage, and build up one another? Do they see people who are committed to what they say they believe? ✧ This is your life. Make it count for Christ.

So What? ✧

- ✧ How hard is it for you to live out your faith? Why?
- ✧ Do you feel scrambled or slow-cooked? Explain.
- ✧ How will you make your life count for Christ?

39. The 180 Factor

Recommended Resource

For a complete program based on this talk, see *Combos: Six Month-Long Themes With the Works* (Abingdon Press, 2004; ISBN 0687740029)

Story idea
(Use this story or a similar one of your own.)

When I was growing up in Mississippi, we had to find creative ways to entertain ourselves. We used to play a game with dirt clods (or "dirt clogs" in Mississippi English). After the cotton was picked and the ground was plowed and a good rain came, God would form these round hunks of dirt. We would go out into the field grab a handful of "dirt clogs," run around, and throw them at one another. It was kind of like redneck Laser Tag.

If you hit somebody below the knee, you got a point. If you hit someone above the knee, you lost a point. Most importantly, if you threw a "dirt clog" with a rock in it you were disqualified. Hitting someone with a "dirt clog" was cool, because it just exploded into a cloud of dust. Getting hit by a rock, on the other hand, would sting like crazy.

The Point: to help youth turn away from sin and toward God

The Scripture: "Woman, where are they? Has no one condemned you? ... Neither do I condemn you. Go your way, and from now on do not sin again" (John 8:10-11).

Start Talking

Let's start with this question: Why do we have messages, prayer time, and worship in youth group? Why don't we just play games and hang out? The answer is of utmost importance! I know there are voices that surround you and tell you, "You are not important. You'll never be good enough." There are voices that say, "Forget God! Jesus is a hoax! Religion is for the weak. Smart people, strong people don't need a god. You need to be cool—get drunk, take this drug, have sex. Do whatever you can to be cool."

Why do I think this time for prayer and worship is so important? Because, for some of you, it might just save your life. For others it might save you from being hurt emotionally or physically. When you are here, you are told that God loves and cares for you; when you are here, you are surrounded by people who love and care about you.

Speak the Word
🖰 **Read aloud John 8:1-11.**

Here's a woman caught in the act of adultery, one of the worst things a woman could do back then. I picture her being half-clothed or naked (after all she was caught in the act), embarrassed, ashamed, bruised, bleeding, scared. She knows that she is about to be killed. The law said she should be put to death by being stoned.

Can you imagine the crowd screaming, "Kill her! Stone her! She deserves to die for what she has done! It's the law!" Can you see the stones in their hands? Even the religious leaders are there, holding stones, ready to punish this woman. And then there is Jesus writing in the sand. What is he writing? Maybe he's writing to the woman, "Have no fear." Maybe he's writing to the religious leaders, "Why are you doing this?" Maybe he's writing the word *LIAR* and drawing an arrow pointing toward one man, or *THIEF* and an arrow pointing toward another. Then he stands up and says, "If you have never sinned, go ahead and throw a stone." Can you imagine the hush that falls over the once wild crowd. Then Jesus writes again in the sand. I think this time he's writing to the woman, "Child of God, I love you!" When Jesus stands again, he and the woman are alone surrounded only by rocks. Jesus asks, "Where are your accusers?" And there are none!

Because she came face-to-face with undeserved, limitless love, this woman experienced "The 180 Factor." Jesus said, "Neither do I condemn you. Go your way, and from now on do not sin again." Think about this: What if a small group of the woman's accusers had stayed—not to throw stones, but to reach down to the woman, help her up, help her deal with her pain, and restore her to the community? That's our project: to create a safe place for hurting people, to demonstrate God's love to everyone.

Close your eyes. Picture yourself doing something that you know is wrong, but that you do regularly. Picture yourself doing the worst thing you've ever done. Picture yourself getting caught. Open your eyes. Do any of you pass the "stone-throwing test?" Are any of you completely innocent?

Many of you know the hymn "Amazing Grace," but do you know the story behind it? It was written by an English man named John Newton. As a boy, John's mother forced him to go to church. He found it boring and irrelevant. When he grew up, he abandoned God and became a slave trader. He bought and sold people as slaves and treated them cruelly when they were in his possession. Many Africans slaves died on John's slave ships. In 1748, he was sailing back to England when a tremendous storm hit. Sailors were swept overboard and water rushed in faster than it could be pumped out. Facing death, John called out to God for help. He doubted that God would help him because he felt his sins were so great that he could never be forgiven. John survived the storm and started reading the New Testament. John developed a relationship with Christ. He realized that he didn't deserve forgiveness and that he could never earn God's love no matter how good of a life he lived. As he surrendered his life to God, he wrote these words:

> Amazing grace, how sweet the sound that saved a
> wretch like me,
> I once was lost, but now I'm found; was blind, but
> now I see.

Wrap It Up

Romans 5:8 says, "God proves his love for us in that while we still were sinners"—thinking the worst thoughts, doing the worst things—"Christ died for us"—for you and for the world.

If you have not experienced The 180 Factor, if you are not a follower of Christ, I want you to close your eyes again and recall the things you have done in your life that you know are wrong. Picture yourself in the middle of the screaming crowd, accusing the woman. What message would Jesus write in the sand for you? If you have had an encounter with Christ and have experienced God's love, maybe you need a fresh message from God. What message is Jesus writing in the sand for you today? Is God calling you to drop a stone and help someone up? Who is it?

So What?

- Where do you find yourself in the story of the woman caught in adultery?
- What do you need to do to experience "The 180 Factor"?

40. Family Feud

The Point: to help youth be the body of Christ at home

The Scripture: "Love never ends" (1 Corinthians 13:8).

Start Talking

Raise your hand if you have the "perfect family." No hands?
Raise your hand if your family could appear on *Jerry Springer*. I
want to challenge you to think about what it means to be a family.

Speak the Word

The Old Testament tells several stories about messed up families.
Remember Joseph—the guy with the colorful coat and eleven
brothers? Joseph's brothers resented that he was their dad's favorite
son. Joseph's brothers were so jealous that they plotted to kill him.
They threw him in a pit and sold him as a slave, then told dad that
Joseph had been killed by a wild animal. That's messed up!

We know that family life is often full of tension, grief, and drama.
Listen to some common complaints from parents and teenagers:

Parents: "Your attitude stinks!"
Students: "You just don't understand!"

Parents: "Do you think that money grows on trees?"
Students: "Why do you ask so many questions?"

Parents: "You're not going anywhere until you clean your room!"
Students: "Why do you yell all the time?"

Parents: "You better check your priorities young man!"
Students: "It's none of your business!"

Parents: "No kid of mine is going to be a slacker!"
Students: "Nothing is ever good enough for you!"

It is easy to get caught up in a family feud. It is very easy to
disappoint and be disappointed. We are all human, but we are also
a family. Let's look at some hard truths about family life:

1. Perfect parents don't exist; babies don't come with directions.

꩜ **2.** This might totally confuse some of you, but you are not the center of the universe. The earth really does revolve around the sun—not you!

꩜ **3.** Your parents don't owe you stuff, and they can't fix all of your problems! Stuff is not the source of true happiness, and life is not always a smooth ride!

꩜ Family life is all about growth, which means struggle, doubt, resentment, and fear. If your family is going to thrive, you have to compromise and make sacrifices. Make having eye-to-eye and heart-to-heart relationships a priority. Be patient, kind, forgiving, honest, hopeful, and generous with your love.

The Simpsons offers an interesting commentary on our society. That show is so funny! But there is a problem—actually multiple problems, but this is a big one—Bart runs the family. Bart despises teaching, direction, and especially correction. But these things are critical for growth—they are signs of loving parents.

Life is a "we thing!" We were not created for independence. We truly were created for *dependence*—on God and on one another. Life doesn't work any other way. We need one another.

Be the body of Christ in your home. Lean on one another. Be humble and flexible. Some people say that trust is the most important attribute of a relationship. But look at Jesus and Peter's relationship. Peter was like Jesus' brother. Yet he denied even knowing Jesus when the heat was on. ꩜ If their relationship had been built on trust, what would have happened? And when Jesus gave Peter another chance, he didn't say, "Can I trust you?" Instead, Jesus asked, "Do you *love* me?"

Wrap it Up

We are called to be a family. The drama and crisis that is present in your family life will also be present here. ꩜ Let's work hard to build our family on love. You have a Heavenly Father who loves you very much! God knows that sometimes life is very lonely and scary. Talk to your Father. I promise that God's loving arms are wide open. [**Read aloud 1 Corinthians 13:1-8a.**] Love never ends.

So What? ꩜

🗨 How is your family like the body of Christ?

🗨 Are your relationships built on trust or love?

🗨 How can this group draw strength from being a family?

Scripture Talks: 50 Creative Messages for Youth

#1. How to Survive Looking Good

The Point: to help youth see themselves as children of God

The Scripture: "Don't worry about *things*—food, drink, and clothes. For you already have life and a body—and they are far more important than what to eat and wear" (Matthew 6:25, TLB).

Start Talking

Today we will focus on how to survive looking good. I'll admit that I am still working on it, so I brought my trusty magazine on "How to Be Sexy" that I got at the grocery store. But first, I want to know who you think is sexy. Guys, who do you think is the best looking female actor? musician? athlete? Girls, who do you think is the best looking male actor? musician? athlete? [List the students' answers on a markerboard or large sheet of paper.]

We've got to make sure everyone likes us. We've got to be popular. But that's not what God says. God doesn't want us to sacrifice what's most important to us to look good for our friends. God doesn't want us to sacrifice our health for beauty. God doesn't want us to sacrifice our futures for five minutes of pleasure. What are you willing to sacrifice to look good?

Story Illustration

(Use your own examples, or say that you heard these from a friend).

We all want to look good. I've worked with some very "good-looking" kids in the past. One was a fifteen year-old who signed a million dollar modeling contract. I was really proud of her. She was beautiful inside and out. She made the cover of *Teen Magazine*! But, my most vivid memory of her was when she was covered with dirt surrounded by twenty of the poorest little kids imaginable on one of our mission projects.

One became Miss March in *Playboy*. She was eighteen years old. Some people tell me that she was a youth group failure. Most of us would love to be the center of attraction. I mean what's wrong with turning a few heads? What's wrong with having nice things? What's wrong with being successful? What's wrong with muscles? What's wrong with implants?

Speak the Word

Don't misunderstand me—popularity, happiness, and success are not bad. I want each of you to have lots of friends and to be happy and successful. But think about what you are committing your life to. How far will you go to be popular or successful?

⏺ Read aloud Matthew 6:25.

The world will tell you that you have to look a certain way, wear certain clothes, and talk a certain talk in order to get ahead. Don't believe it. Surround yourselves with true friends who can remind you of who you are, even when being yourself is difficult. You need a place to belong—like home and youth group. Trust God to meet your needs, because sometimes people will fail you.

I love the show *Survivor*. One of my favorite cast members was Dirk Been. Contestants could bring one "luxury" item to the South China Sea. He brought his Bible! When he got voted off the island, he left his Bible behind in case anyone needed it.

Sounds crazy doesn't it? He could have brought anything, and he brought a Bible. I am sure people all over the world said, "That guy is stupid!" But it poses an important question: If you are a Christ-follower, how does your life show that this Christianity stuff is real to you? Where is the evidence? ⏺ How does your life look different because you follow Christ?

Wrap It Up

How often are you concerned with how you look as a Christian? What if you paid more attention to your Christian witness than to your outward appearance? Outward perfection is not the goal of Christianity. Some people make a mistake or wrong choice and give up on faith. The truth is everybody makes mistakes— sometimes big ones. ⏺ Hear this: God says, "I love you no matter what! You are beautiful in my eyes. Don't let the world tell you any different. I will take good care of you."

So What? ⏺

- ✺ How much pressure do you feel to look good?
- ✺ What does God think about your outward appearance?
- ✺ How could you spend more time on your relationship with God than on your looks?

42. Operation

The Point: to help youth let Jesus take away their pain

The Scripture: "See what love the Father has given us, that we should be called children of God; and that is what we are" (1 John 3:1).

Start Talking

I love the game Operation®. Operation® requires patience and a steady hand. If you touch the side, an annoying buzzer goes off and you lose your turn. I played it all the time when I was a kid—long before X Box™. Back then, I wanted to be a doctor. Though the sight of blood grossed me out, I wanted to help people.

Maybe some of you have had operations. I've had two. They were necessary to remove bad parts, to remove the sources of hurt. All of us have things that need to be removed from our lives.

Speak the Word

1 John 1:8 says, "If we claim to be without sin, we deceive ourselves and the truth is not in us." Aren't you glad people cannot see all the thoughts that float around in your head? Hiding the bad in our lives is in our best interests. We want to look good. We want to at least *appear* perfect and problem free. We fear disapproval. We are afraid that if people see our shortcomings, they won't like us, much less love us. We are embarrassed by our feelings, and we hide. Some people hide for so long that they forget they are hiding at all. What about you? Have you been hiding for a long time?

This self-deception causes guilt, self-hatred, feelings of inferiority, confusion, shame, hopelessness, and even addiction. The world piles on the hurt, saying, "You'll never amount to anything!" This stuff must be removed so that we can really live.

Everyday, our culture tries to make us forget who we are. Our struggle against the dominant culture is intense. We feel pressured to be popular and powerful. When this pressure is combined with poor self-image, bad decisions are right around the corner.

Too often, the applause of others drowns out God's voice. To please others, we don't say what we truly believe. We end up hiding from God just like Adam and Eve. Here's some truth to hold on to tightly: ✝ What remains hidden cannot be healed.

How many of you think God loves you only because God has to? Too many of us have trouble being honest with God. We feel that, if God knew the truth, the love would be gone. We feel this way because this is how we act: Someone hurts us, and we remove our love. We do the same to God. We reduce God to some old man who is nothing more than a bookkeeper of wrong doings.

We often project onto God our feelings about ourselves. If we hate ourselves, we assume that God also feels hateful toward us. We project onto God our views of our parents. Authoritarian parents yield a punishing God. Loving parents yield a loving God. When we do not love ourselves, accepting love from others is difficult, if not impossible. Believing that God could love us is even more difficult. When we can love, forgive, and accept ourselves, it is easier to love, forgive, and accept others.

Sometimes we get so busy trying to prove that we are worthy of love that we don't hear God telling us how precious we are. We wear ourselves out. We beat ourselves up with the past as if this earns us spiritual brownie points. Hear this! No matter what you have done, God loved you in the past and promises to do so for eternity. ✝ No amount of spiritual makeup is going to make you more presentable to God. Only the sacrifice of Jesus can do this!

✝ Read aloud 1 John 3:1.

Jesus wanted to show us where we stand. Jesus wanted us to know that God is our Father. God is intimate, not distant; caring, not removed; family, not dictator. Jesus frees us from negative voices. Jesus frees us from ourselves.

Wrap It Up

If you allow him, Jesus can be your surgeon and remove the hurt, the things that keep you from living. ✝ Jesus can help you dare to live as a child of God. Every other identity is an illusion.

So What? ✝

✦ What do you hide from God?
✦ What do you need Christ to remove from your life?

Michael Williams
*is the pastor of
Blakemore United Methodist
Church in Nashville,
Tennessee and the writer and
editor of the* Storyteller's
Companion *series (Abingdon
Press).*

*Michael is also a certified liar, having
won the Liar's Contest at a national
storytelling competition. An amazing
story writer and storyteller, he can
make you feel like you're sitting in
the Garden of Eden watching the
whole story unfold or like you're
standing in one of the crowds
surrounding Jesus. The stories in
this chapter are meant to be
memorized and told like
monologues. They will make
great additions to your
talks and Bible
studies.*

43. A Taxing Journey

It is bad enough to have to pay taxes, but to have to travel in order to register to pay taxes is even worse. Especially at a time like this. Mary could have her baby at any moment. She shouldn't have to travel the roads from Galilee to Bethlehem. She shouldn't have to go anywhere at a time like this. Governors don't care about things like that, though. They just want their money, and they want to be sure everyone pays.

I am no governor, anyway, just a simple woodworker. I try to make a living for myself, my new wife, and this child that is on the way. My son, for we have been told that the baby will be a boy, will grow up to know the smell of cedar and the feel of woodworking tools. He will have wood shavings in his hair and nicks and splinters all over his hands. He will study the Torah and grow up to be a scholar and a fine upstanding man. May he live to see his children's children. That is my prayer for my son.

I say my son, though he technically isn't mine. He belongs to God, his mother tells me. The rabbis say that it takes three to make a baby: a mother, a father, and God. I felt very left out at first, since I will not be his father by blood. But I will be his father by love, I can tell you that. After all, every child really belongs to God. It's just that Mary and I realize that fact more than most parents.

When Mary first came to me with the news, we were just engaged. She told me about an angel who spoke to her, and God's breath surrounding her, and that she was going to have a child, but it was really God's holy spirit. My head spun. It didn't make any sense to me. All I could think of was that my wife-to-be was going to have a baby, and we weren't even married. What would the neighbors think? What would our families say?

I would never hurt Mary for the world. I wanted to believe her, but I had never heard of such a thing happening. No one else had, either. I decided to end the marriage contract very quietly. Then she could go live with her relative Elizabeth and have the baby there. I did not want to put her—or myself—to shame.

Little did I know that I was next in line for a visit. One night as I lay sleeping, I dreamed that an angel appeared to me and told me not to be afraid. I should go ahead and marry Mary, the angel said. She had told the truth; the child was God's own beloved child. I was to have the honor of raising God's chosen child. To tell you the truth, it didn't feel like such an honor at the time. All I could think of was the way people would shake their heads and make mean comments behind our backs—or to our faces.

Time has changed my thinking, though. I married Mary, and I am proud to be her husband and the child's "stepfather," I guess you might say. We are married, and I will raise him as my own son. Not all the people have changed their way of thinking, however. When I found out we were going to have to travel to Bethlehem, I contacted all my family who lived there and asked if we could stay with them. Surprisingly, everyone of them had already filled every spare sleeping space. There was not a single place for Mary and me.

I honestly don't know if my relatives were telling the truth or if they had heard that Mary was having a baby and had counted the months between our wedding and the time the baby was to arrive. Perhaps they just didn't want us staying with them with a baby on the way so soon. Perhaps they thought it would bring shame on their family just to give us a place to sleep. As I say, I do not know.

Still, that means that we have no place to stay in a city that will be filled with people. I am sure that every inn will be filled, and those that aren't will take one look at this poor woman about to give birth and suddenly find that they just filled the last sleeping space. Then what will we do? I don't know. I will just have to worry about that when we arrive.

For the first time in my life, I have an idea of what those who have no homes to go to feel like. I have seen them begging for a crust of bread in the streets all my life, but never had I been able to imagine what their lives are like. Never to have a place to get in out of the rain or the cold. Never to know the welcome of a family waiting for you, or a cooking fire that has your supper kept warm above its flames. I will tell my son the story of this journey so that he will always have a kind heart toward those who have no place to go. As Jews we are required to give alms to the poor, but this story will assure that he always does it with a heart of love.

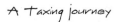

A Taxing journey

My other worry is how I will ever find a midwife for Mary when the time comes. In Nazareth I would know who to send for. In Bethlehem I have no idea who will help us. Will I have to help Mary deliver this child?

It's unheard of! I wouldn't know how to begin. I don't think a woodworker is made for such important work. I'm sure I wasn't. I will ask for a midwife as soon as we arrive, just in case we need her. Should the child be born, on our journey, it will just make another fine story to tell this special child about his birth. Even the worst things that happen to you in life make good stories, as soon as the pain and worry have gone from them.

"What's that, Mary? Yes we have many more miles to go. I know you don't feel well. Here, lean on my arm as we walk."

I have to remember she is hardly more than a child. She never expected to have her life turn out this way. Neither did I, but I am older and have seen more difficult times than Mary. If I could carry her on my shoulders, I would.

"How much longer? I don't know. We will stop and rest along the way whenever you need to. Here, don't cry, my dear Mary. All will be well. Just wait and see. The child will wait for us to return to Nazareth. He will be born at home, and we will name him Jesus, just as we were told. Your family will surround you, and you will have plenty of help."

I feel like I could cry too. What will become of us? To the Romans we are just another number on the tax rolls. To our families we are just another couple that could not wait until they were married to have a baby. The angel told us that we were the ones God picked out to bear the Chosen One into the world. To ourselves we are just another couple trying to get through the day, making a taxing journey into a future only God knows. God, help us on the way.

"Yes, my love, let's stop here and rest. Whatever happens, God is with us."

From *Bible Zone Older Elementary 6* [1998] Abingdon Press. Used by permission.

Scripture Talks: 50 Creative Messages for Youth

44. An Angel

I guess it is because I am young, as far as angels go, that I get such different and interesting assignments. My name is Gabriel, and I was just starting out when the story I am about to tell you took place. Though it happened a long time ago, these events are as fresh in my memory as if it had all taken place yesterday.

One day God sent for me. I knew it was important because all my assignments up until that time had come through other, more experienced angels. Angels are all God's messengers, but not all of us get our messages straight from the mouth of the All Compassionate One. Only the most high-ranking assignments come directly from God.

I'll be honest: I was very nervous coming so close to the Creator of the Universe, but the other angels told me that God really puts you at ease as soon as the two of you meet. I found that it was true. Walking into God's presence was like entering a warm, lighted room after having trudged through a dark, cold winter's night. I looked around expecting to see a fireplace, but soon came to realize that the light and warmth all radiated from the place where God was standing. I say standing; but I could just as well say hovering. You see, God doesn't always appear the same way, even to angels. Sometimes there will just be a great light; at other times a gentle father or a strong mother; at other times a rock or a whole fortress. God seems to appear to mortals and angels in the way each can best understand.

"Gabriel," God said. Even the voice was comforting. "I have a very important message for you to deliver, the most important in all of what humans call history. You are to go to a young woman who lives in a city named Nazareth in the region called Galilee. Her name is Miriam*, and she has been chosen to bear my child. My spirit will surround her like a cool breeze, and she will discover that she is going to have a baby. This will come as a shock to her at first. That's why I want you to go tell her whose child it is she is carrying and what a blessing he will be to all people.

*Mary

"There is another thing I want you to do. Miriam is engaged to be married to a man named Joseph. This will come as unwelcome news to him, since they are not yet married and have never lived together as husband and wife. He will not want to hear what you have to say, but you must explain the situation to him in a way that he can accept."

"Why me?" I blurted out. "Why would you entrust me with such an important message?"

"The young woman is very young, little more than a girl. I didn't think you would frighten her as much as some of the more experienced angels. Some of them can be terrifying, you know."

I did know. I knew I must do everything I could to put Miriam at ease as completely as God had done for me. I was given the rest of the details of the message. Then God ended our time together by saying, "Shalom. Peace go with you, my young friend."

So that is how I found myself standing in the room of the young woman Miriam in Nazareth of Galilee. God was right; she was little more than a girl. I had practiced my opening line all the way. I wanted it to be serious enough for her to realize that the message was important, without scaring her half to death.

"Greetings, O favored one. The Lord is with you." I thought that sounded like a good beginning, serious but not scary. I said it in the most gentle voice I could, but she turned and stared at me with such a terrified look on her face that I quickly added, "Don't be afraid, Miriam. I'm not here to hurt you."

The girl didn't look like she believed me, the part about not hurting her, that is.

I wanted to put her at ease. "You may find what I have to tell you hard to believe, but you have found favor with God. You are going to have a baby, a son, and you shall name him Jesus. He will grow up to be very great and will be called Son of the Most High. God will place him on the throne of his ancestor King David. His reign will not end like those of other kings, but will never end."

At least Miriam was beginning to look more stunned than frightened. "How can that be? I'm not even married to Joseph yet." I couldn't tell if she was talking to me or to herself.

Scripture Talks: 50 Creative Messages for Youth

So I completed my message with this explanation: "God's spirit will surround you like a breath of wind, and God will cast a long shadow upon you, so your child will be a holy child, the Son of God. Even as we speak, your relative Elizabeth, who everyone said could never have a baby, is going to have one in three more months. You see, for God nothing is impossible."

After a long silence Miriam spoke, "Here I am, God's servant. It is fine with me if everything happens just as you have told me."

She had understood and even more. She had accepted her assigned role in this divine drama. But would Joseph accept the situation? That's another story.

After a time word came back to God that Joseph had been told that Mary was going to have a baby. He took it better than everyone expected, since he knew that he could not be the father. He decided to quietly put an end to their engagement, so he would cause as little embarrassment as possible to both families. God sent me to convince him to go ahead and marry Miriam. This would be an even tougher job than breaking the news to Miriam. He wasn't a young girl, after all, but a grown man.

First I decided to appear to Joseph in a dream. After all, I had read Genesis and knew that his ancestor Joseph was good at interpreting dreams. My fear was that he would not take me seriously, so I used my deepest, most authoritative voice. "Joseph, son of David," I began. I have to say it did catch his attention. "Don't be afraid to marry Miriam. The baby she is carrying is the child of God. You will name him Jesus. He will be called this because he will set the people free from the prison of their sins. The prophet Isaiah said it all, 'A young unmarried woman will have a child, and her child will be called Emmanuel, which means 'God is with us.' "

I wasn't at all sure that he believed me until I heard that Joseph had married Miriam and that all was taking place just as it was supposed to. I'm really glad I was able to do the assignment God had given me.

From *Bible Zone Older Elementary 6* [1998] Abingdon Press. Used by permission.

An Angel

45. At the Pool

"Do you really want to get well?" He had the nerve to ask me that. "Do you really want to get well?" He said it as if I really didn't want to get well.

I did, you know—want to get well, that is. Anyone who had been unable to walk as long as I had would want to get well. For thirty-eight years I laid by that pool at the Sheep Gate. For thirty-eight years I had wanted to get well. I'm sure that at least at the beginning I wanted to get well. I was just a boy.

I had come to that pool in the first place because of the story. The story I heard was that sometimes an angel came to the pool. You couldn't see the angel, but you could tell it was there. Suddenly the water would begin to bubble. Then it would start to churn. The angel was stirring the waters, they claimed.

At first I thought the angel had jumped right into the pool and was splashing around in the water. When I told the others what I imagined, they laughed at me. They told me that the angel only leaned down and stirred the waters with its hand. Those who gathered around the Sheep Gate told me that the first one to get into the pool after the angel stirred the waters would be healed.

The waters don't stir very often and never at the same time of the day or night. So people hang around and wait. They wait for the angel. They wait for the waters to begin to bubble and churn. They spend their lives waiting. Then when the waters would begin to move, people would scramble for the pool. There were arms and legs everywhere. Sometimes people were injured worse trying to get into the pool than they had been before.

From time to time some joker would catch everyone off guard, a little sleepy, not paying close attention. Then he would dip his hand quietly into the pool and begin to make splashing sounds just to see the people scramble.

I became one of those people who waited. Why would I have waited, if I didn't want to be healed? I could not move from my waist down. Since I had no one to put me into the pool when the angel stirred the waters, I had no chance to be healed. Then he came along. I had no idea who he was, or why he was asking me questions. There were plenty of sick people at the Sheep Gate. Why did he pick on me? He seemed to know I had been here a long time. I couldn't help it. I had waited. I had tried. It wasn't my fault I wasn't well.

Then he asks, "Do you really want to get well?" as if I didn't. I tried to explain about the pool and my legs. I tried to tell him that I had no one to help me, but he didn't seem to be listening to my story. He continued to look directly at me. Then he said, "Take up your mat and walk."

At first I couldn't believe what I was hearing. "What?" was all I could say. What a cruel thing to say to someone who hasn't walked in thirty-eight years. As if I could just make up my mind to get up and walk.

"Take up your mat and walk." I felt a tingle in my feet. It had happened before. I would think I was feeling something, but it was just my imagination playing tricks on me.

"Take up your mat and walk." The tingle became a pain. My feet and legs began to hurt. I tried to move them, and they actually moved.

"Take up your mat and walk." I tried to get up. It had been so long since I had used my legs that I couldn't remember how to walk. It felt like I was about to topple over at any moment. I made my painful way through the crowd. I looked for him; and would you believe it, he was nowhere to be found.

I walked around, my legs still stiff from lack of use. I began to think, Now that I could walk, people would expect me to find work. I had never worked; I had only waited. It was all I knew how to do. As I walked through the streets, I made quite a sight. Some religious leaders saw me and recognized me from the pool. They asked me if the angel had stirred the waters. I told them, "No."

Then they asked me what had happened. I told them that someone had told me, "Take up your mat and walk." And I did. They seemed angry and said, "Who dared to heal you on the sabbath?"

To tell you the truth, I had forgotten that it was the sabbath. So much had happened so quickly. I just wasn't thinking.

"I don't know who he was." It was all I knew to say. It was the truth.

Later I went to the temple to look around. I didn't really know how to pray. I was too busy waiting for the angel to stir the waters to pray. Then I saw him. The people standing around me told me that his name was Jesus. When he saw me, he walked over, looked me in the eye, and said, "You are well now. Be careful. See that something worse doesn't happen to you."

I was beginning to wonder if getting well was such a great thing after all. Walking still hurt. Since I didn't do it very well, it made me stand out in a crowd. Now it seemed something worse could happen to me. I went straight to the religious leaders who had asked and told them that it was Jesus who had made me take up my mat and walk. And, yes it was on the sabbath.

They went directly to the place Jesus was teaching and accused him. I stayed back at a safe distance where I could not be seen. When they accused him of healing on the sabbath, his answer was as strange as his comments to me had been.

"Did you or did you not heal on the Sabbath?" they asked.

"My Father is still at work, and I am still at work," was all Jesus replied.

Did he mean that God was his father? Did he mean that he was God's son? Was he talking about them both being at work on the sabbath, or just at work generally? Was he giving credit to God for the healing?

I don't know the answer to any of these questions.

From *Bible Zone Older Elementary 5* [1998] Abingdon Press. Used by permission.

46. Three Ways of Looking at a Healing

THE MAN: I was so scared, I was willing to go anywhere, talk to anyone, do anything. My twelve-year-old daughter was near death. What at first seemed to be a slight illness got worse and worse. Finally she just lay there. It was hard to tell if she as breathing at all.

I had heard of a rabbi who was known to have healed people. He was a Galilean named Jeshua*. He had a small but devoted following. It didn't really matter where he was from, or how well-known he was. I was going to beg him to make my daughter well.

When I found him, he was talking to some of his followers. I interrupted, stopping him in mid-sentence. "Please, sir. My daughter lies ill at my house. She is near death. Please come with me. I'll give you anything if you will only save my daughter's life." I begged. I pleaded.

He looked at me with great sympathy. He simply nodded and began to follow. We hadn't gone ten steps before one of my servants came running up to us. "There is no hurry now," he shouted. "She is dead. She died a short time ago."

I could feel the agonized cry escape my throat. No sooner had he heard my cry than this Jeshua placed his hand on my shoulder. He turned me to face him and looked into my eyes. Tears were already making their way down my face. "Don't worry," he said with assurance. "She's not dead. She's only sleeping."

He said this with such confidence that I continued to walk toward home. How could he have known that my daughter still lives, while my servants who had seen her thought she was dead? I couldn't think about that. I kept repeating to myself with every step. She is not dead. She is only sleeping. She is not dead. She is only sleeping. His words carried me home.

THE WOMAN: For twelve years I have been losing my life. If blood is life, then each day for that long time my life has been draining away. I am weak, and my skin is as pale as wood ashes.

*Jesus

Worst of all, my suffering leaves me alone. My blood makes me unclean, they tell me. No one will come near to me for fear that they might accidentally touch me and become unclean themselves. For fear of becoming like me, they avoid me.

I had heard of a man from Galilee named Jeshua. He is a teacher and healer. I have heard that he even allows women among his followers. I am sure that anyone who gets close to him will be healed. I intend to be healed.

I watched and waited. He was always surrounded by a crowd. I could never get close enough. Then one day I was watching, hoping for any chance to get close.

A man came running up to Jeshua. He was clearly upset. He spoke quickly, almost pulling the teacher along with his voice. Jeshua followed, and for a brief time the crowd around him thinned enough for me to find a place in it.

I moved in quickly, but the teacher was walking fast, and I could not reach him. Just then, though, some other men stopped their progress. As they talked, I saw my chance. I reached out and touched the hem of his cloak. I heard his voice before I felt anything change. "Who touched my clothes?" The teacher turned and locked my gaze with his eyes.

"In a crowd like this? How can he tell?" His followers did not know that he had already found me. As the teacher looked at me, I knew that the bleeding had stopped. What all the physicians could not do, he had done. I was clean.

"Daughter," he called me, "your faith has made you well. Go in God's peace. You are free now." And I was.

THE GIRL: First I was hot. Then I was cold. Then I was hot again. I would awaken. Then I would sleep. Then I would dream. Then I would wake. Then I would sleep again.

In my sleep there were wild beasts chasing me. There were giant insects who trapped me in dark corners. I was falling, falling, and falling again, always waking before I hit the ground.

Sometimes I thought I could hear my parents calling for me. I don't know if they were really calling to me or if I was imagining it all. I didn't hurt anywhere. I wasn't comfortable, but nothing hurt that I could pinpoint. I felt bad all over, but there was not a particular pain anywhere.

Then here was the light. It was warm and yellow and washed all around me. I could look straight at the light, and it did not hurt my eyes. It was as much like warm water as it was like light. It made me feel warm and comfortable and loved.

Love, that's what it was—a feeling of such strong love that I wanted to go deeper into it. I felt as if I was walking deeper into the light.

Then I heard the voice. It wasn't the voice of one of my parents, but it was a voice that held so much love in it. At first I wasn't sure whether I was being called deeper into the light or back into my life. Soon I began to understand the words; "*Talitha Cum.*"

"Girl, get up," it kept repeating.

Slowly I felt myself rising. The light became more and more dim, but the feeling of love was as strong as ever. Before I knew what was happening, I was sitting up talking to a man I had never seen before. It was his voice that had called me back to life. He told me his name was Jeshua. He didn't talk to me as if I was a child. He talked to me as if I was his friend.

From *Bible Zone Older Elementary 5* [1998] Abingdon Press. Used by permission.

Three Ways of Looking at a Healing

47. A Special Love

Rabbis always sat down when they had something important to say. When Jesus saw the crowds of people following him, he found a spot on a hillside where he could see everyone and they could all see him. His closest students came and sat near him so they could catch every word. When he was sure everyone was in place, Jesus began to teach them about God, saying:

"God has a special love for those who are poor in their spirits. God has a special love for those who feel like they have no friends. God has a special love for those who don't get presents on their birthdays or whose birthdays are not even remembered by anyone. God has a special love for those who lie awake at night in fear or who wake from nightmares. God has a special love for those who are afraid to go out during the day and whose lives are living nightmares. In God's reign all of these will live under God's royal protection.

"God has a special love for those who have experienced a death in their life. God has a special love for those who mourn the death of a loved one or the death of love itself. God has a special love for those who grieve the loss of their youth or the loss of their home or the loss of their own sense of who they are. God has a special love for those who walk around breathing but feel like they are dead inside. God has a special love for those who can't feel anything but how much it hurts to be alive. God will put an arm around their shoulders and comfort them as only a friend can.

"God has a special love for those who are meek, who stand by the wall waiting for someone to speak to them, but no one does. God has a special love for those who are hurt by others but have no voice with which to express their pain. God has a special love for those who have a deep concern for others, but no one will listen to them. God has a special love for those who live at the edge of other people's lives so long that after a while they become invisible. God has a special love for those to whom no one ever says, 'Thank you.' God will take up for them and see that they get the very best that the earth and life has to offer.

"God has a special love for those who long to love God as much as they hunger for something to eat and thirst for something to drink. God has a special love for those who want to do the right thing, even when they aren't quite able to do it. God has a special love for those who try their best to love even those who don't love them in return. God has a special love for those who want God for their best friend. God has a special love for those who do not recognize that God is already their best friend. God will come to even those who yearn for God's friendship without knowing what it is they are yearning for, and give them what they need.

"God has a special love for those whose hearts are filled with mercy and whose lives are filled with kindness. God has a special love for those who speak a kind word when others speak harsh words to them. God had a special love for those who touch others tenderly instead of striking out at them. God has a special love for those who overlook the failings of others, even when those failings cause them pain. God has a special love for those who are kind when it would be easier to be mean. God will surround them with mercy and kindness in return.

"God has a special love for those whose hearts and lives are so pure you can see right through them. God has a special love for those who do not misuse the good gifts God has given them. God has a special love for those who do not fill their bodies with things that will harm them. God has a special love for those who want to do what God wants them to do. God has a special love for those who want more than anything to see God. They shall see God.

"God has a special love for those who make peace in their lives and communities. God has a special love for those who stop arguments before they start. God has a special love for those who look for common ground with those who disagree with them.

"God has a special love for those who refuse to bear weapons against those with whom they disagree. God has a special love for those who refuse to use even words as weapons. All these are called children of God.

"God has a special love for those who suffer because of their love for God. God has a special love for those who are called terrible names because of their love for God. God has a special love for those who are physically hurt because of their love for God. God has a special love for those who are excluded because of their love for God. God has a special love for those who keep company with those who are called terrible names, who are physically hurt, who are excluded, or who suffer in any way because of their love for God. All these shall have a special place in God's reign."

Then Jesus continued, "God also has a special love for those who suffer because they are my followers. You can be glad when this happens, because that is the same way people a long time ago treated the prophets. So you see, you are in good company."

Jesus taught his followers many other things which they remembered and by which they tried to live.

From *Bible Zone Older Elementary 6* [1998] Abingdon Press. Used by permission.

48. A Worthy Soldier

He was a soldier of the army that had occupied her homeland for so long that it seemed like they had been there forever. The soldiers were generally hated by her people. Many were cruel and ordered the locals around like they were their own personal slaves. She didn't hate them, but she didn't have much to do with them either.

Some of the women in her church had come to her asking a favor for the soldier. His servant was sick, and the army doctors could not do anything for him. She wondered why he had sent for her.

The women who came said he was a good man, even if he was a soldier. He had been nice to the people at their church. He attended sometimes and always put something in the collection plate. When the roof needed repairs, he not only helped pay for them, but he also helped the men make shingles and put them on the building.

She was well-known as a healer throughout the county and beyond. She knew which herbs to gather and how best to prepare them. Some could be chewed directly. Others worked best when made into a tea. Still others she could make into a poultice to place on hurt areas of the body.

Every now and again she would be called on to use a gift that had been passed down from her father—she would stop blood. When someone would send for her saying that a friend or relative had fallen or had been badly cut on some farm implement, she would go into a room alone and open her Bible to the portion her father had shown her years ago. Then she would read the passage over and over again as she imagined the stopping of the flow and finally the clotting of the blood.

She was not allowed to tell anyone which exact passage of the Bible she read. If she did, she would lose the gift. She could pass it along to some younger male relative before she died, as her father had passed it along to her. She had to give the gift to a male in the next generation as her father had given it to her, a female. These were the rules of the gift, and she didn't dare break them.

When the women from church arrived, they were out of breath. They had run most of the way, and these were people who were not used to running.

"Saidie," they called. "Somebody needs you quick."

"What's the matter?" she asked them.

"There's a soldier." The words were spoken through the labored breathing of those who had just run farther and faster than they were used to. "He has a servant. The servant fell. He's bleeding. The soldier is a good man, the one you see in church. Can you help?"

"I'll help," she answered. "Take me to him."

"Can't you do it here?" they wanted to know.

"I can," Saidie responded, "but I can do it there too. Come on."

She walked quickly with the women until they reached the soldier's camp. She passed through the other soldiers like they weren't there. When they arrived at the soldier's tent, he was pacing outside.

"Thank you for coming," he said. "I didn't want to send for you at first. I didn't want you to think I was trying to take advantage of you."

"Not at all," Saidie answered. "I want to help if I can."

"I'm a captain, and I am used to giving orders and having them followed. I hope you don't feel like I'm trying to order you around in this case." The captain sounded sincere.

"If I thought you were trying to order me around, I would not have come. Now, where is your servant?" Saidie followed the captain into the tent where a young man, hardly more than a boy, lay. There were bloody rags wrapped around his head, and he appeared for all the world like he was dead.

"Leave me with him," she told the captain.

After the soldier had gone, Saidie knelt down by the servant's cot. She opened her Bible to the familiar place and began to read to herself. She moved her lips, but no sound came out, as if she were trying to protect from someone overhearing and trying to take the secret.

Minutes passed. She began to hear the boy's breathing become regular. She leaned over him and unwrapped the blood-soaked rags that lay about his head. There were crusts of dried brown blood along each ear canal, but there seemed to be no fresh bleeding.

"Bring me some water," Saidie called out. Moments later the captain entered the tent carrying a basin filled with water and some clean cloths. He stood beside the cot and watched as Saidie cleaned the servant boy's head up. After a thorough washing you couldn't tell that he had been injured at all, except for a purple bruise on his temple.

"He's going to be all right," she told the captain. "He just needs to take it easy for a while."

As they walked outside the tent, they saw the women from church who had been waiting for some word on the servant's condition.

"He'll be all right in a few days," Saidie told them.

"How can I ever thank you?" asked the soldier. "Can I pay you something or give you something?"

"You don't owe me anything," Saidie said quietly. Then she raised her voice so the whole group could hear. "You are supposed to be my enemy. You, a captain with the army that occupies my homeland. But, you know, I have never seen such love and faith and decency in my own people as I have seen in you. Anything you ever need from me, you just ask."

With those words she turned and motioned for the other women to follow her. As she walked away, she heard the captain's voice. "Thank you. You're a gift from God, you know that?"

From *Bible Zone Older Elementary 5* [1998] Abingdon Press. Used by permission.

49. Gripe, Gripe, Gripe

"I hate it here," Rachel complained, "Why did we ever have to leave home?"

"This is our home now, Rachel," her grandmother's voice was quiet and calm, "We must learn to live here, to make it our home."

"But we had it so much better back in Germany. Here we have to learn a new language. The food is not the same. Our clothes are not the same. Nothing is the same. I hate it." Rachel's voice was anything but calm.

"It always takes time to get used to a new place. You know we can't go back to Germany. There people spit on you and call you. bad names. There we would have to wear a yellow star on our clothing. If we were still there, we all might be dead now. God had blessed us by bringing us to New York."

"But Grandmama," Rachel insisted, "There we had a house; here we have to live in Uncle Moishe's apartment with his family."

"We are blessed that your Uncle Moishe is willing to take us in." Grandmama gathered Rachel into her lap and stroked her hair as they talked. "We have something to eat each day. We have a place to sleep that is warm and dry. And, most important, nobody is trying to kill us."

"I know, Grandmama," Rachel told her. "It's just so hard for me to learn everything I need to know to live in New York."

"Being free is always hard," Grandmother explained. "This is not the first time the Jewish people have had to flee a wicked ruler, and it is not the first time we have had to learn the difficult art of freedom. A long time ago, before there was a man named Hitler, there was a king named Pharaoh. This king kept the Jewish people as slaves until God brought us out of slavery with a mighty hand.

"And do you know what was the first thing they did when they got safely on the other side of the sea?" Grandmama asked.

"What Grandmama?" Rachel loved hearing her Grandmother's stories from long ago.

"They did exactly what you were doing a minute ago. They started to complain. Gripe, gripe, gripe was all they seemed to be able to do. 'We had it better as slaves in Egypt,' they said. 'There we always had food to eat,' they said. They must have forgotten that they were only fed so they could be worked to death. 'Did you bring us into the wilderness to kill us?' they asked Moses.

"So God, who had gone to so much trouble to bring them out of Egypt, was repaid with complaints rather than gratitude. So what did God do?"

"What?" Rachel was really interested, especially since she had just been complaining herself.

"Did God punish the people?" Grandmother continued.

"Did God punish those who complained?" Rachel, the complainer's, question was serious.

"No, my little complainer. God fed them instead. Each evening quail would fly into the camp for their dinner. Each morning they collected the bread of heaven that God provided for them. They didn't know what it was, so they called it manna, which means 'What is this?' "

"What did it taste like?" Rachel was beginning to get hungry.

"The Bible doesn't say what it tasted like, but the rabbis say that manna tasted like the thing you were most hungry for. If you liked sweet rolls, it tasted like sweet rolls. If you liked chicken soup, it tasted like chicken soup. If you liked chocolate, my little one, then I suppose it tasted like chocolate." Grandmother knew that chocolate was Rachel's favorite.

"If it tasted like chocolate, I would have collected a truck full." Rachel's eyes sparkled at the very thought of that much chocolate.

"Oh, you couldn't do that. You could only collect as much as your family needed for that one day. Of course on Friday you could collect twice as much, enough for the sabbath, too. If you tried to gather more than you needed, it would spoil. You see, when God feeds you, everybody has enough and no one has too much."

"Is that why Uncle Moishe goes to the grocery every day, so his manna won't spoil?" Rachel asked.

"Perhaps that's it, little one." Her grandmother smiled back at her.

"There's one thing I don't understand, though. The people complained and God fed them?" Rachel rolled the thought around in her mind.

"That's right, little one, that is the kind of God we worship. God may be angry with us for a moment, but God feeds us every day. It's called steadfast love, God's steadfast love endures forever." Grandmother smiled as she said this.

"That's kind of like your love, Grandmama," Rachel added. "You feed me every day, even when I complain."

"Don't forget Uncle Moishe," Grandmother told her. "He welcomed us into his home and gives us food here. He is well named, don't you think? Like the Moses of old."

"Did the people ever complain again?" Rachel asked.

"Plenty of times," Rachel's grandmother said. "It seems that freedom is a difficult thing to get used to. Sometimes people get so used to their slavery that they prefer it to freedom. When you are free, you can't just blame other people for your troubles. You have to take responsibility for yourself."

"Grandmama, I hope it is a long time before I have to take responsibility for myself." Then Rachel added quickly, "I'm not complaining. I just hope you will be with me a long time."

"So do I, my little Rachel. So do I. Now do you think we should get some of those sweet rolls that Uncle Moishe brought from the grocery for us?" Rachel's grandmother laughed.

"Yes," answered Rachel, "but just enough for today."

From *Bible Zone Older Elementary 5* [1998] Abingdon Press. Used by permission.

50. Decisions, Decisions

Moses wasn't really sure who he was. His name was Egyptian. Moses means "son of." Tut-Mose meant "Son of Tut." Ka-Mose meant "Son of Ka." Who was Moses? Son of whom. The Hebrew woman who nursed him and helped raise him had taught him the stories and customs of the Hebrew people. After all, he was a Hebrew.

All the same, he was groomed to be a prince of Egypt. He was schooled in Egyptian language and thought. He learned Egyptian customs and wore Egyptian clothing. He knew Egyptian laws that allowed Hebrew slaves no rights at all.

How could he decide who he was? If he decided to be an Egyptian, he would be a person with certain rights and powers. He would have the respect of other Egyptians and would be feared by the Hebrews. If he decided to be a Hebrew, he had nothing to look forward to except hard work and an early death. He would be foolish to embrace his Hebrew roots.

Sometimes, though, one decision leads to another, then that decision leads to another, and pretty soon we wind up someplace we never expected to go. That is what happened to Moses, son of no one.

One day Moses was walking around a construction site. Hebrew slaves were busy making bricks by mixing mud and straw, packing the mixture into rectangular forms, then putting the forms into the blazing Egyptian sun to bake and harden. Egyptian overseers watched to make sure that the slaves continued to work without stopping. They carried whips with which to beat the slaves and used them whenever the Hebrews displeased them.

Moses happened upon one of these overseers beating a Hebrew. The overseer showed the slave no mercy, and it appeared that he would kill the slave before he was finished. Moses had to make a decision. Would he stop the overseer from beating the slave? What reason would he use? Slaves had no rights.

Moses decided to remain as calm as he could and to take a practical approach. "You know if you kill that slave, Pharaoh will have two fewer hands to do his work."

"What business is that of yours?" growled the overseer.

"I just don't want you to get into trouble for slowing down the work by killing that slave." Moses' voice was becoming a little unsteady, but he tried to hide its shakiness.

"Mind your own business. What are you, a Hebrew yourself, or just a Hebrew lover?" The Egyptian would not stop beating the slave.

What would Moses have to do next? He could feel the anger rising in him. His face was hot, and his throat was tight. He thought he would hit the overseer and knock him out. Then he could take the slave to safety before the Egyptian woke up. When the overseer turned away from Moses, the young Hebrew raised his hand to strike the cruel Egyptian. His hand came down with greater force than he intended. Perhaps he was angrier than he realized. A sharp pain shot through Moses' hand when it struck. The blow made a sickening thud. The Egyptian fell down and lay still.

Moses looked to see if anyone had seen what he had done. Then he helped the slave back to his co-workers, who took care of him. When Moses returned to the Egyptian, he was still lying face down. It was clear that the overseer was dead.

Now Moses had another decision to make. Would he just run away or try to hide what he had done? The young Hebrew decided to dig a shallow grave in the sand and to bury the dead man there. Moses was sure no one had seen him.

The next day, though, Moses passed by a couple of slaves who were fighting. He tried to stop them.

"Don't the Egyptians kill enough of you? Do you have to try to kill each other?"

"You're a good one to talk," one of the slaves shot back. "Do you think that you are Pharaoh now? What are you going to do, kill us like you did the Egyptian overseer?"

Hearing that, Moses knew he had to make another decision. Did he dare stay and take the chance that Pharaoh would never learn

Scripture Talks: 50 Creative Messages for Youth

that he had killed an Egyptian? Or should he run away to some place beyond Pharaoh's reach? If he didn't get away now, would he ever escape?

Well, Moses decided to escape as soon as he could. He made the right decision. When Pharaoh learned that Moses had killed the Egyptian overseer, he ordered that Moses be killed.

Now, Moses' decisions had cut him off from the two people who might have told Moses who he was. Moses could no longer be a Hebrew or an Egyptian. He left both behind and became a man without a people. Now he had to decide where he would live.

Moses traveled to a land called Midian. He stopped by a well, and there he met seven young women keeping their family's sheep. Some other shepherds wanted to keep them from watering their sheep. Should Moses step forward to defend them? After all, they were not his people or his family. It wasn't his business.

Still, he hated to see people take advantage of others. Moses decided to take up for the young women, and they were allowed to water their flock. When they returned home, they told their father, Jethro, of the kindness that a stranger, an Egyptian, had shown them.

So Moses was invited to eat with the family. Before long he married one of the young women he had met by the well. Her name was Zipporah. Moses became a shepherd, keeping sheep for his father-in-law. It was a good and simple life. There were few decisions to be made beyond where to graze and water the sheep.

Moses' life now was not at all like his life in Egypt. He never expected to see Egypt again, and never expected to be faced with those difficult decisions again. But you know, one decision usually leads to another.

From *Bible Zone Older Elementary 5* [1998] Abingdon Press. Used by permission.

Scripture Index

Scriptures   Talks

Scriptures / Talks

Scriptures   Talks

Topic Index

Numbers refer to talks that deal with each topic.

Scripture Talks: 50 Creative Messages for Youth

Scripture Talks: 50 Creative Messages for Youth